W9-AYE-457

Written in Blood

COURAGE AND CORRUPTION IN THE
APPALACHIAN WAR OF EXTRACTION

Edited by Wess Harris

*A portion of the proceeds from the sale of this
volume will be used to preserve the stories the
Whipple Company Store has to tell.*

Written in Blood: Courage and Corruption in the Appalachian War of Extraction
Compiled and Edited by Wess Harris

This edition © 2017 by Appalachian Community Services and PM Press

ISBN: 9781629634456
LCCN: 2017942905

Cover by John Yates/stealworks.com
Cover photo of the 1968 Farmington Mine disaster © Bob Campione
Interior by Jonathan Rowland

10 9 8 7 6 5 4 3 2 1

PM Press
PO Box 23912
Oakland, CA 94623
www.pmpress.org

Appalachian Community Services
229 Birtrice Road
Gay, West Virginia 25244

Printed in the USA on recycled paper by the Employee Owners of
Thomson-Shore in Dexter, Michigan

Contents

Acknowledgments

THIS CUSTOMARY AND OBLIGATORY PAGE OFFERS AN OPPORTUnity to thank those who have made a work possible while absolving them of any blame for errors of the editor. Consider it done. Special gratitude must be shown to two groups whose work does not physically appear herein.

In recent years countless miners and descendants of miners have offered stories and documents that supplement and confirm the tales in both *When Miners March* and this small volume. In addition to purely substantive contributions, their encouragement has been invaluable on those days when the task has seemed too great. Dwight Siemiaczko is a relentless researcher of all things Paint Creek. Kathryn Bowles offered her great-grandfather Bill Derenge's autobiography. Terri Whitlock, granddaughter of Clarence E. "Red" Jones, provided the "smoking gun" that confirmed Van Bittner's sellout of the Union contracts. Elwood Maples saved documents that would have been lost forever. J.W. Sheets II stepped up and shared his grandfather's treasure so that future generations can see as well as read their history. Joy and Chuck Lynn refused the bribes offered to sanitize our history and at great personal expense have insisted on letting the Whipple Company Store tell its stories.

Unlikely and somewhat unwelcome heroes can also be found at Radford University. Radford has agreed not only to house but also actively manage the William C. Blizzard/*When Miners March* collection. Much of the primary source material for both *When Miners March* and this work can now be accessed at the Radford University Archives. Candidly, this is most unfortunate. These materials should ideally be kept within the state of West Virginia, but that is not possible. Not one of the three institutions in West Virginia that might reasonably be expected to have the physical capabilities to house and preserve this incredible collection has the academic integrity to be trusted to tell the miners' tale and make it available to future generations. Sad but true. Researchers wishing to continue primary source research are directed to Radford.

Words cannot capture the gratitude I feel to those whose lives are celebrated in these pages. They are the true heroes. Thanks and bravo as well to the selfless scholars who contributed time and talent to making this book possible. Shame on those who made it necessary.

Introduction

THE GREAT MINE WAR OF WEST VIRGINIA HAS NOW RAGED FOR over a century. Most of the battles recalled here occurred in the state and most contributors are West Virginians. Yet war seldom adheres to lines neatly drawn on a map, so events in neighboring states on occasion find their way to these pages. The coal miners of West Virginia are central to the tale, yet the tale is much larger indeed. Ranging far beyond a battlefield narrowly defined, it is the story of America and its people. Who are we? Who have we been? Who will we become? Who decides?

Much has been written about the "mine wars" of the early twentieth century but only recently have we come to realize that the discussion is not about mine wars—Cabin Creek, Paint Creek, Blair Mountain—but about a single war between the people of West Virginia and the interests of King Coal that stretches from those early battles to current struggles to save the Union so many fought and died for years ago. This small anthology focuses on more than a century of conflict. The struggles, defeats, and victories are ultimately part of a much larger war. The war is between those who would make their homes here and strive to see our land survive and prosper, and those representing the interests of large capital seeking to maximize profit. Notably, in Joe Manchin, we have a senator, former governor, and coal broker who does not hesitate to remind us that we are an "extractive state." As the coal industry faces inevitable decline, the war continues pitting the local population against those who see new fortunes to be made by extracting our natural gas treasure while leaving only polluted land, air, and water in exchange for short-term employment opportunities. Incredibly, the most precious resource extracted from our state has been our people. Wave after wave of economic refugees have been forced to first move to the industries of the North and later to the nonunion

1

2 Written in Blood

jobs of the South. Each departing youth further weakens the remaining population in our ability to resist the extractions . . . the destruction.

We share this small volume not as a magnum opus on the men and women of the coalfields but as a collection of unique offerings seeking to stimulate thought and discussion of our history. It is often noted that the "winners" get to dictate the record of the past. Despite a massive effort to spin the tale to the contrary, the writers in this collection refuse to accept defeat. Indeed, we believe that an honest look at events through the lens of the decades reveals a past in which we find "a lot of the little things the great people did, and a lot of the great things the little people did" (*When Miners March*, p. 382). While we place an absolute priority on scholarly accuracy, no attempt is made to match the dry style of learned journals. "This is a people's history, and if it brawls a little, and brags a little, and is angry more than a little, well, the people in this book were that way, and so are their descendants" (*WMM*, pp. 381–82).

The trajectory is all too clear. The power of wealth that gave us the robber barons—Collins, Carnegie, Rockefeller et al.—led inevitably to Esau in the coalfields. While history books record these gents as cultured philanthropists, perhaps it is more insightful to ask: How far from the abuses of the Esau system to the unpunished, overlooked murders in Farmington? From Farmington to the industrial homicide at Upper Big Branch? To the ecocide and unemployment caused by the destruction of our mountains and water? Why do we not hear demands for trials for crimes against humanity and reparations to pay for the damage done? Going beyond the shills for the interests of capital, the future of Appalachia, of America, demands we look with both eyes open to our past and into our future. Both eyes must be open and our glasses must not be custom-tinted by those seeking to keep us in the dark. Understanding requires an accurate look at our past and clear glasses—solid theory to interpret the facts as we discover them.

In the spirit of searching for truth, we ask you to join us in this commitment to take back our story and the cultural institutions now in the service of extractive industries. We invite public officials to find the courage to cast off the burdens of censorship and join us in this effort. Together we can lift the dark veil smothering the truth, authenticity, and humanity of our past. Only then can we look beyond the hopelessness and bitterness of defeat to a sense of genuine belief in a better future . . . after the war is finally ended. It is time to speak truth to power. It is time to speak truth to our children.

—Wess

Away with pious references
To patriotism and to prayer,
As the naked child is born,
Let the truth lie cold and bare!

If there is a thing to tell
Make it brief and write it plain.
Words were meant to shed a light,
Not to cover it up again!
—Don West, 1950

"Hard times are coming, when we'll be wanting the voices of writers who can see alternatives to how we live now, can see through our fear-stricken society and its obsessive technologies to other ways of being, and even imagine some real grounds for hope. We will need writers who can remember freedom."
—Ursula K. Le Guin

Esau in the Coalfields
Owing Our Souls to the Company Store
Michael and Carrie Kline with Joy and Chuck Lynn

Originally published in a slightly different form in Appalachian Heritage (vol. 59, no. 5, Summer 2011).

ÉMILE ZOLA WRITING OF WORKING CONDITIONS IN THE FRENCH coalfields of the late nineteenth century penned vivid pictures of coal camp life that resonated deeply with mining developments in the new state of West Virginia during the same period. This fiction, based on Zola's six months of intensive research living and taking careful notes in the coal mining district of Borinage, in the Alsace region of northern France, featured such familiar themes as child labor, appalling working conditions, hunger, ever-mounting debt at the company store, crippling and maiming from industrial accidents, and early death from industrial diseases. In *Germinal*, Zola explored another mortifying interaction between the company store and the village women and girls, daughters and wives of the coal miners: "It was a known fact that when a miner wished to prolong his credit, he had only to send his daughter or his wife, plain or pretty, it mattered not, provided they were complaisant."

In West Virginia we have our own versions of child labor, appalling working conditions, hunger, ever-mounting debt at the company store, mine guards, Gatling guns, and labor wars. But until quite recently, the use of female flesh to extend credit to feed the family was never mentioned by our own regional historians. We've pretty well accepted that early coal operators were a mean, iron-willed breed bent on ruthless control and rising profits—but surely not that mean.

Zola's *Germinal* was published in 1885. A year or two later the young Collins brothers arrived in the Fayette-Raleigh coalfields of southern West Virginia from their home in Alabama, where Justus Collins had gotten his start in personnel management overseeing prison labor in the mines around Birmingham. These young adventuring capitalists soon bought into thousands of acres of rich coal lands just as the new industry was emerging in the raw and lawless wilderness of our state. So successful was Justus Collins in this land of opportunity that in just a few years he had built and was operating three octagonal, turreted company stores in southern Fayette County, the Justice Colliery Company Store in Glen Jean, the Collins Colliery Company Store in Prudence, and the Whipple Colliery Company Store at the intersection of Rt. 612 near Oak Hill, West Virginia. These stores serviced the needs of families employed at the various Collins mines. The store at Glen Jean burned to the ground in 1934, the year of Collins's death. The same fate befell the Prudence store a few years later. But the Whipple Store, completed in 1893, has miraculously survived for nearly 120 years, a kind of social/industrial history vault in which many unspeakable secrets are stored.

This past July 4, my wife Carrie Kline and I had a prearranged date with Joy and Chuck Lynn, owners and interpreters of the Whipple Company Store Museum and Learning Center these past five years. They bought the imposing old building when it was on the verge of being condemned and razed. Recently retired from business in Florida, they were attracted to the aging structure because of all the history lived within its walls for more than a century.

Joy and Chuck agreed to take us on a tour of the building, even to show us the old embalming room in the basement which was in constant use from when the store was completed in 1893 until the federal government instituted the death certificate in 1932. We recorded their compelling interpretations, moving from one room to another throughout the long day. Our conversations began on the high, arched porch overlooking the parking area and roadways below.

The initial glaring question, of course, was why would two people entering their retirement years want to take on the co-lossal task of restoring and preserving this relic of the gilded era of coal company dominance. The more than 6,000-square-foot structure is in desperate need of a new roof, for starters, and, of course, heating and plumbing. The list of needed repairs is formi-dable. Joy Lynn explained that taking on the company store was more to her than just a passing fancy.

Joy Lynn: "My mother is a coal miner's daughter, and my grandmother is coal mining family all the way back to the begin-ning. Mother was raised nearby on the New River in Brooklyn. I was born in Oak Hill Hospital just two miles up the road, and Granny has been here all her life. Mother has been back and forth between Brooklyn and Michigan. I guess this is really a rescue project. The roof is in bad shape. But with the amount of history surrounding this building, tearing it down was something I didn't want to see happen. Restoring it as a museum was a project we wanted to take on."

The Whipple Company Store was completed a couple of de-cades into the burgeoning coal and timber rush in the wake of the American Civil War. Soldiers from invading armies of the North had gone back home after the War with tales of the huge trees and rich outcroppings of coal. Surveyors and engineers soon came for a closer look.

For a clearer sense of how this land and resources grab played out in Fayette County and beyond, I reread Ron Eller's *Miners, Millhands, and Mountaineers: Industrialization of the Appalachian South, 1880–1930*. The fine-toothed precision of Eller's research makes for troubling reading. The chaos and looting of the re-gion's natural wealth and environmental splendor was akin to the feverish activity of mad dogs in the sheep with blood on their fangs. The new social order that rose to power between 1880 and 1930 quickly abbreviated the U.S. Bill of Rights in industrial communities that they built and controlled, and took care of business with ruthless, self-proclaimed authority. In many coal and timber producing counties, venture capitalists with small armies of mine guards built their own courthouse towns—and courthouses—to baffle existing systems of law and order. Controlling the assessor's office and county land records were essential steps in the ever-expanding development of mills, mines, and railroads.

The vast influx of outside wealth in the 1880s and 1890s financed the passing of an old pre–Civil War order rooted in the rawness of the frontier, a well-defined local power structure dating to the times of earliest settlement. Now an invasive species of colonizers was having its way with local traditions of leadership and displacing a diverse, agrarian, largely bartering economy with rail transportation, industrial wages, Gatling guns, and a cash economy conducted through the company store.

Suddenly the remote vastness of the southern Appalachians buzzed with new industrial enterprise as European immigrants fresh from Ellis Island flooded into boomtowns and labor camps to join contract labor from the cotton fields of Alabama and local men and boys from hardscrabble farms scattered throughout the hollows and hillsides of the region.

Chuck Lynn: "The men coming here from Ellis Island, of course, [were] getting caught up in the system before they arrived. They got a train trip from Ellis Island down to here and were in debt to the company the minute they stepped off the train. Of course they'd be paid in company store scrip. They'd never have cash to send for their families overseas.

"The company would provide the new arrivals with carbide lamps and tools needed to start work. During the Depression immigrants were hoping to get work in their field if they were stonecutters or in the laboring trades. So they get off the boat and there's somebody saying, 'We'll give you a trip to where there are plenty of jobs and good living conditions and—oh, there's just a few catches along the way.'

"On election day the people who collected the ballots in most cases around here were the mine bosses. So the bosses handed out a ballot already filled out and ready to sign. If the miners didn't sign it, they would lose their jobs and get thrown into the streets. That's how the bosses kept all the politicians under control."

Construction of railroads penetrated the bountiful commons of the Appalachians to coincide with the opening of mines and lumber mills. In Fayette County coal and timber development followed the Chesapeake and Ohio Railway, completed through the New River Gorge in 1873. Coal mining companies could timber up a heading and open a mine for very little investment. Before they could go to work shooting and loading coal, miners were impelled to build the infrastructure that made possible the removal of coal from underground, placing timbers and laying track without pay. They had to buy the tools with which to mine the coal. They were paid only for the coal they loaded—and the company did the weighing.

But even with all this easy access to untold fortunes and totalitarian control of their workers, the coal operators feared unions and unionizing activities in adjoining states and beyond. After the economic slump of 1893, the nonunion coalfields of West Virginia emerged on the national coal market with a decided edge over Ohio and Pennsylvania dogged with labor troubles and crippling strikes. Production rose astronomically in West Virginia over the next few decades, as the state's natural wealth was hauled away to the Great Lakes region and beyond in coal trains that always came back empty.

The Whipple Company Store has maintained an iconic connection with that era for almost 120 years. It is a flash point for local memory. And the man who built it, Justus Collins, driven by fears of organized labor, was determined to keep the union out of southern Fayette County. Forever. With that in mind, he designed the store primarily as a fortress and staffed it with armed operatives posing as clerks and spying on customers while filling their orders from shelves behind the glass counters.

Joy Lynn: "He called it the Whipple Colliery Company Store. Whipple was his wife's family name. She was Lucy Whipple Dent Collins [with Georgia roots], and their daughter was Amy Whipple Collins.

"Justus Collins designed his company store as a security system. It wasn't built for beauty. It was built so the company owners and the company store workers could hear and see everything. Back then the only form of security people had were the guns they were toting, and their eyes and ears. Justus Collins brought the Baldwin-Felts men here from Bluefield and from the coal mining companies that he owned near Pocahontas."

Lon Savage, author of *Thunder in the Mountains: The West Virginia Mine War 1920–21*, reports in *The West Virginia Encyclopedia*:

> The Baldwin-Felts Detective Agency played a controversial role in the early years of the coal industry of southern West Virginia, enforcing public law at the direction of coal operators who hired them. Their often brutal, repressive policies, especially toward union miners, contributed significantly to the violence of the period. From the beginning, Baldwin-Felts agents were deputized by hard-pressed local sheriffs to maintain law and order, but coal operators increasingly used them to prevent organization of the miners by the United Mine Workers of America. The guards kept

union sympathizers from entering the coal camps. They spied on miners, reporting those with union sympathies, their highly organized spy system extending even into the UMWA leadership. In 1902 they helped break a strike in the New River Field. Eventually, their overriding purpose in West Virginia was to prevent unionization of the miners.

Joy Lynn: "Those men could stand hidden behind the bases of the arch on both sides of the front porch, stand there with guns, look in the windows opposite, and look out into the road in front of the company store. So the windows were strategically placed for that reason. The original wooden steps were very steep and narrow, no handrails."

The steep and narrow access would have made it difficult for more than a couple of men to rush the building at one time. Armed to the teeth, the guards were strategically placed to handle whatever threats the workers might pose in the heat of strikes or other disputes. The Whipple Store was a no-nonsense, state-of-the-art design for labor management at every imaginable level. It was a metaphor for the owner's resolve to keep the union out. It was fortified to protect the interests of an occupying owner class, and its staff of mine guards was capable of unleashing well-directed armed force from within if ever it became necessary to do so.

Joy Lynn: "So they monitored who came in and out. Women were primarily the shoppers in the company store. They actually enjoyed themselves and could converse with one another."

Joy recalls how eager her family was to get the store opened as a museum and learning center after they acquired it in 2006. At the time of the opening in May 2007, the last whispers of local memory about the fragile old structure were still audible.

Joy Lynn: "We decided to open in spite of the condition of the building because most of the people who could give us any history would be in their late seventies, eighties, and nineties. We've already had quite a number of people who lived this history come back here as visitors to the building. They've been giving us specific stories about their experiences here. I try to write people's comments after every tour so I can get as much of it documented as possible."

With her round, open face and friendly brown eyes, Joy Lynn invites confidences and sharing. Like Kanzeon, the Buddhist incarnation of compassion, she hears the cries and painful recollections of a troubled region. As a recipient of so many memories and testimonials, Joy explains her system for evaluating what she hears.

Joy Lynn: "Older people from surrounding communities come in here to tell me what I don't know. They often think that because I'm 'just a young girl' I can't possibly know anything about this, because they've lived it. When they tell me their stories, they get a dot on the wall and they get their story written down. When I have three dots I tell the story to others."

By triangulating what she hears, Joy has been able to develop an interpretation for the museum based on details that bubble up from her conversations with local visitors. These revelations are always stunning—often painful—and as a curator of local memory she is respectful of what she hears.

Joy Lynn: "We have had people coming in here whose mothers had to go through very hard times to raise them. They don't want that publicized. Some of the things are humiliating. And they made these sacrifices because they nurtured and cared about one another. They lived in these small communities by themselves and were governed by coal owners. People talk about how awful it was, but many people come in and tell stories about how life was so good. They cared about one another. They loved one another. They watched each others' backs."

The Whipple Company Store sold everything from canned goods, clothing, and crowbars—to live canaries. The birds were sold in little wooden cages and accompanied the miners to their workplaces underground. The tiny lungs were fatally affected by poisonous gasses, and the birds' sudden death warned the miners of the presence of odorless "black damp" in the underground room.

The old freight room's entrance is to the left of the porch and its floor-to-ceiling shelves are full of mining memorabilia. Some of the items were left behind with little interpretive information after the store closed in 1954, and it has been the Lynns' quest to learn from local visitors about the terminology and function of some mining equipment from earlier times. Some details are hard to hear. Joy points to a small aluminum dinner pail on a nearby shelf.

Joy Lynn: "This little mining bucket here we just had a recent story on. I didn't know anything about the dinner bucket. I called it a little kid's picnic bucket. A gentleman came in last year with his grown children and grandchildren. He had been a miner for fifty-some years. With his family members crowding around, he was telling them about all this equipment, and the canary story, and about the mine boss, and the children going in the mines. He finally turns to me, points to that dinner bucket, and he pokes me in the arm and he says, 'Little lady, tell me about that bucket.' I says, 'Well, sir, I don't know anything about that bucket.'

"He says, 'When you lived in the coal camps back early on, if your daddy got killed in the mines, your mama had to pack up and leave. There was no ifs, ands, or buts. She was out, out, just out. But if she had a young boy eight or older, he could mine in place of his daddy, and that way his mama could stay in the mining camp.' The old gentleman went on to explain how you'd give the children eight to twelve years old those smaller dinner buckets to keep with them at all times. That way the men who were more seasoned miners would be alerted to a young boy that might need some help. Or if they needed their back watched in the mines, maybe that young miner wasn't the right person to choose. Those boys tagged along behind men who might educate them.

"So I told him, I said, 'Sir, that's a great story, but I've never seen any documentation about smaller-sized dinner buckets. I haven't seen them in photographs.'

"And he says, 'I can show you my dinner bucket, because I went in and mined for my mama when I was nine years old. Happiest day of my life was when I turned thirteen and all the men on my shift bought me my man bucket. And I still have both of them.'

"A man and woman came in yesterday, and she told me, 'That dinner bucket story's true. There's a lady that lived four doors from us and said her little nine-year-old boy was in the coal mines.' So a child working down in the mine was doing his daddy's work.

"Their dinner buckets, of course, were very important pieces of mining equipment. Most of the historic photographs of old coal miners show them holding their dinner buckets. We explain about what it meant when a miner poured his fresh water out on the ground. A lot of men who went into the shafts had safety issues about conditions underground, and when they couldn't get the ear of a mine boss or somebody to pay attention to their complaint, they would pour their water out, and all the men would walk out of the mines. That was always a signal, water poured out of their canteen meant that no one goes back in the mines until the problems are resolved. Saved a lot of lives that way."

In the center of the stock room is a six-by-eight-foot freight elevator, hand powered with a thick rope that passes around a large iron pulley wheel at the top of the sixty-foot shaft.

Joy Lynn: "We use it for everything from the basement to the ballroom. It's still 100 percent functional. This elevator seats firmly into the basement floor downstairs, and the double doors on the west side of the building open up. Any kind of pony carts or trucks could back into the area down there and unload onto the elevator. They would bring their merchandise up to this floor to be [inventoried] and put into the company store.

"The elevator would then continue up to this little secret second floor, which doesn't look like much more than a closet. It's about five feet tall and you would unload back this way over our heads. Coffins would've been stored up in that area until 1932. They didn't want women to see anything like that. They needed coffins every day, because we lost mining men in large numbers to mine accidents and occupational diseases. And the coffins would service three mines in the area. Some days they'd need forty, some days they'd need ten, some days one, and some days sixty. We're talking about the period between 1893 and 1930."

The final upward destination of the elevator is the third floor ballroom, which provides rare insights into the social lives of the new owning class in Fayette County in the 1890s.

Joy Lynn: "The ballroom on the third floor is my favorite space, Justus and Lucy's ballroom. What you're seeing is the original 1893 room. Lucy chose gold colors from the West Virginia state flag to accentuate her lavender gown. The door [off the front side of the ballroom] is Lucy's 'ballroom adornment room.' The ladies would go in there and they would fix their hair or maybe their boot and garter. The room with the white door was where the men withdrew for a last smoke before they came out to dance. These men were coal owners and they would meet here because they didn't want people to know what they were doing. [With the threat of violence everywhere in the region], coal owners had to stay kind of in the background.

"Organ music would begin to play as men and women would come greet one another in the center of the dance floor. These elite dancers preferred waltzes. Ballroom floors were often suspended back in the 1800s because a slightly bouncy floor put a bounce into the step of the dancers."

The design also gave Collins and his detectives an acoustic structure for the surveillance of all spoken conversations in the store downstairs.

This level of control by the company men reached into every nook and cranny of the miners' lives. The threat of terror and level of fear in the daily lives of coal camp residents was palpable. Civil rights were unheard of. For more details on the kinds of challenges these conditions posed for union organizing, I turned again to W.C. Blizzard's *When Miners March*, edited by Wess Harris and based on firsthand accounts of the labor wars, especially the Battle of Blair Mountain, which rocked the West Virginia coalfields into the 1920s. Fayette, along with other southern coal mining counties, was repeatedly under martial law. The ever-vigilant company operatives were always on the watch for union organizers.

Chuck Lynn: "The Baldwin-Felts guards were not all carrying guns. Some of them were miners. Some of them were local law officials, sheriffs on the company payroll. So any talk of unionizing would be nipped in the bud. The men would be immediately fired."

Joy Lynn: "We don't have any pictures of the inside of this building. We have one inside picture of Justus Collins's twin store over in Glen Jean. It burned in 1934. It shows us this counter, which is one of the most important features of this building. It is architecturally [designed as] a security system. This gentleman is a Baldwin-Felts detective. He posed as a clerk. Women were primarily the ones with information about the union meetings, because they were the ones here shopping and visiting with one another."

But with the acoustic design of the ceiling, even low-level conversations bounce off the concrete walkway to the ceiling and back to the center of the store.

Joy Lynn: "This guy behind the counter can hear you. No matter where you are."

In the gilded age of the mining industry, companies re-cruited a diversity of workers from many parts of Europe, the agricultural fields of the Deep South, as well as the surround-ing hills and hollows of the mountain region. Justus Collins was a pacesetter in hiring a diverse labor force. Historian Ken Sullivan wrote: "Collins's comment that mine managers should strive for a 'judicious mixture' of races and nationality groups, on the theory that diversity hampered unionization, is often quoted."

Joy Lynn: "Justus Collins had them all segregated in such a way so that they couldn't communicate with one another. If you came here and talked a foreign language, and you lived with the foreign language–speaking people, how're you going to learn English? You don't. So you can't understand; you can't band to-gether; you can't unionize.

"The black people [experienced] intense segregation. Before the union came in, black people in Whipple lived directly behind the store, where soot [from passing C&O locomotives] would come down on them. The white people lived up above, and they had the white school. [In order to get to their own school each morning], the black children would have to cross paths at the white children's school and of course get beat up on a daily basis. We've had black people come in and tell us that.

"Blacks weren't allowed in the company store except at cer-tain times on certain days. They had a window on the side of the building. They would hand their list in. The clerk would take care of everything and then hand it back out the window. Only certain days and times they were allowed in here.

"Everyone was kept separate. 'Hunk Hill' was across the street. Anybody who didn't speak the language was a 'hunky.' It didn't matter what nationality you were, German or Polish, Czechoslovakian, Hungarian or Italian. Those are mainly what we had here. And there were many single men coming from

Ellis Island, no family, nobody. They'd stick those men into more dangerous areas underground. Nobody was accounting for these people.

"And when you hear the stories about how the miners were expendable and mules were more important than the men, it was because the men didn't cost anything. But those mules were expensive to replace."

A little later on in the afternoon, we fumbled down a long, dark stairway into the basement where Chuck Lynn joined us for a closer look at the dark underbelly of the Whipple Store.

Chuck Lynn: "This room here was the embalming room, a room inside the basement, but with windows. So it's a straight pass through rather than bringing bodies in through the front door. The embalming service was in operation up through 1931. The miners' burial fund was a deduction from their check. If they didn't have their burial fund up to date or were a newly started employee, then the cost of their coffin would have been deducted from their last paycheck before the family would get anything. This is where they would have dealt with the bodies of miners who died anywhere in the coal camp. I imagine there were several bodies handled through here from uprisings or any mine wars. There are many unmarked cemeteries around here where the bodies would have gone."

Carrie Kline: "What did you mean 'uprisings or mine wars'?"

Chuck Lynn: "The many mine wars: Paint Creek, Cabin Creek, and of course Blair Mountain, where the mine workers retaliated against the mine owners. They would go on strike. They would be thrown out of their company housing and forced to live in tents until they came to terms with the company. A lot of times they didn't, and of course the company would bring in other workers to substitute for them, other 'scab' workers, they would call them in the union field, to live in their houses and work their jobs for the same, or even lower, wages than they were being paid. Pretty rough life. But if you abided by the rules, put up with the situation and pay, you did fine.

"The Paint Creek Strike [of 1913] came up as far as Dothan just up the road from here. And a lot of union miners from here marched on Blair Mountain in 1921 because this was all union territory at the time. But then again, it wasn't a strong union. The coal owners could decide whether to abide by union demands, or just completely ignore them."

The rapidly expanding coal and timber economies, well-oiled with state and federal subsidies and other tax breaks, made their own rules. They built their own towns with company schools and churches. The coal camps and workplaces were patrolled by company guards. Free assembly of the workers was strictly forbidden. The company doctor saw the workers, heard their complaints, and told them to go back to work. The companies called the shots, maintained their own police forces, and even minted the coins with which they paid their workers. The "scrip" they issued was good only at the company store. The store itself was a fortress constructed to buttress company control against possible infiltration by union organizers and ideas of collective bargaining. Such total control by a few at the top flies in the face of American democratic ideals as guaranteed in the Bill of Rights for every citizen. Throughout the coal mining industry and its communities of workers, at the time the Whipple Store was built in the early 1890s, a system of serfdom and wage slavery was already well established. But humiliation went even deeper.

Just off the ballroom on the third floor of the store is a smaller room toward the back of the building. In early photographs it's the only curtained room. It served as a fitting room, so it has been frequently told, where women were accompanied by one of the guards from the first floor to try on shoes they had seen displayed in the shoe department. A woman, of course, seldom had money of her own and barely enough scrip or credit at the company store to cover the week's groceries and rent. So when she got up to the shoe room she found it furnished with a cot upon which the guard encouraged her to sit while trying on the shoes. When the door shut behind her, she found herself alone with the guard.

Joy Lynn: "Over the past several years we've had eight or ten women refer to this as 'the rape room.' After they got their lovely shoes they would have to pay for them in this room. Then they would be escorted back downstairs to resume their shopping, or pick up their children down there, or what have you. They would have to keep their mouths shut tight about what had happened to them upstairs. If the miners would get wind of this, what would a husband do? How would he react? First thing he would do is react, most men. But if the men were belligerent, they'd soon have 'accidents' in the mines, and we've had reports of that as well. So the women had to do what they had to do and keep their mouths shut.

"One woman comes in and tells me a story. She says, 'I know about that shoe room, because Mama had to go into the shoe room once.' And she says, 'Mama wouldn't buy shoes anymore after that. She wrapped her feet and made her own cardboard and newspaper shoes. And that's all she wore the whole time they lived in the camp.' The daughter was eighty-two years old who told me about her mama's shoes."

Three years ago Joy Lynn had an unexpected, eye-opening visit in the Company Store one day from a woman who had spent much of her professional life working in the bookkeeping office with access to the first-floor safe.

Joy Lynn: "As she tells me her story of working for many years in this office she points out the wear of her own shoes on the floor. She describes stepping up to the door of the safe, which was installed in 1907 by the New River Company. The man inside hands her two guns, which she puts in the pockets of her apron. Then she goes to her desk where she spends the day keeping necessary records for coal miners, and she would meet them at the window, as her business required. The safe stored the bookkeeper's guns along with moonshine and liquor, tobacco, and rolling papers. It also housed morphine and other medications, pay envelopes, mining maps, as well as paper scrip over five dollars. She said this safe was where they would keep the paper scrip and, pointing to each shelf as she described its contents, she was explaining what everything was.

"And she suddenly pointed to five mysterious pieces of paper I had been storing on the shelf under glass and said, 'You've got Esau!' Now I didn't know what she was talking about, so I'm listening. I said, 'What is it?' And she said, 'You shouldn't have that. That shouldn't be here. You don't need to have that.' I said, 'Oh. Well, can you tell me what it is?'

"'Well,' she said, 'it was the way women were administered food.' I said, 'Oh, well, how did they do that?' Because these little white company-issued chits were dated 1922 through '25, '27, in that era. She said, 'Well, sometimes the men would get sick and couldn't mine coal, and the women would need to have food for their children. So the superintendent would administer this for them.' So I asked, 'How would the women pay that back?' They didn't have the ways and means to pay for much of anything. But they wouldn't let their children starve. 'You need to get rid of that,' she said again. 'I don't think you should have that in here. Let me take it.'

"I said, 'No, that's okay. I'll take care of it. Let's go on and look at something else.' And later we got a few minutes alone on the porch. I said, 'You know, I'd really be interested in a little bit more information on how that paper scrip was administered and how the Esau was paid back.' She said, 'Well, you really don't want to keep that back there, because you might have some women come in here, and that will be upsetting to them.' I said, 'Well, I don't really understand why it would be so upsetting. Women make sacrifices all the time to feed their children. That's not so unusual.' She says, 'If a man could get back to work in the mines in thirty days, and he was a good miner, the woman wouldn't have to pay it back.'"

Though penniless and often with her family facing possible eviction, a miner's wife nonetheless possessed physical assets which the Baldwin-Felts guards and other company men at the store often found compelling and greatly desirable. Esau was a kind of super credit issued by the company store superintendent only to mothers of hungry children. The name of Esau comes from the sad story in Genesis, the Twenty-fifth Chapter, in which Esau, a starving hunter, staggering into his brother's tent, begs his brother Jacob for a bowl of beans. Jacob feeds his brother, but only after forcing Esau to sign away his birthright.

For the miner's wife, forfeiting on the Esau agreement meant submitting to the sexual depredations of the company men, compromising her own integrity and birthright, all for a poke of beans to feed her children or a week's rent to keep a roof over their heads. She perceived herself without options, totally victimized by a well-established, bureaucratic system conducted through the company store at a time when corporate profits were mushrooming: the black gold rush of the eastern mountains. But corporate ethics and responsibilities had yet—and still have yet—to be defined outside the caldrons of raw profiteering. Such excesses were built on a system which kept the workers' pockets empty and their spirits broken, the starved-out circumstances in which Esau found himself when Jacob demanded his birthright in return for a bowl of beans.

That bureaucratized rape has been a feature of capitalist expansion and industrial development in the coalfields was a shocking revelation to me when I first heard about it fifteen years ago. A retired coal miner in eastern Ohio recorded for me childhood memories of a "Polish patch," a mining camp in the shadow of a huge tipple. He told me that after his dad was injured in a slate fall underground, his mother had to go in person to the superintendent's office to make "other arrangements" when she could no longer pay the rent on their company house.

I still wonder how widely the term "Esau" has been used to describe this pervasive practice throughout the Gilded Age of West Virginia's beloved robber barons, for whom we have named our towns, colleges, churches, hospitals, and banks, yes, especially banks, throughout the region. What has been the imprint of this totalitarian takeover of the past century and a half on our present social and environmental dilemmas? Would you think that a coal operator who would send an eight-year-old boy to work in his deceased father's place in an underground mine would hesitate to take advantage of the boy's mother? How does what our foreparents went through continue to hang upon our present generation a "company store" sense of ourselves? Old, established patterns of capitulating to company demands, selling ourselves short, even voting against our own best interests, have followed us into presently troubled times. This despondent pattern reflects the oppressive conditions over time of a one-industry economy owned and operated by and for the benefit of outside interests. It's a lot of baggage to carry, a dark image to try to shake off.

Even now we daily give up our birthright for a bowl of Esau beans: a minimum wage pay check at McDonald's, a shift of dangerous work in the bowels of the earth, a bag of prescription pain pills, or very modest subsidies from our currently exploding oil and gas boom. Think about what our overlords have taken from us in return for these crumbs.

Much of the responsibility for these gulag conditions in West Virginia's early development lies with the many administrations of state and local government presiding over the past century and a half of extractive corporate management by outside interests. Our elected leadership has overseen the transfer of ownership of the region's natural wealth from local family deeds to foreign interests. Our leaders have always promoted our state as being "open for business" and upheld the excesses of the coal industry as models of bullish progress, a source of commerce and jobs, despite thousands of industrial deaths and degraded landscapes. Over the past century and more, many public officials charged with safeguarding the interests of their constituents began instead rubbing shoulders with captains of the incipient coal industry, paving the way for out-of-state money men and freewheeling practices.

In *Miners, Millhands, and Mountaineers*, Eller notes one memorable exception to the wholesale accommodation of wealthy entrepreneurs by willing public servants: an 1884 report by the West Virginia Tax Commission. This document warns local citizens that "non-residents are carrying off the most valuable resources of the state, threatening to leave West Virginia in the near future despoiled of her wealth and her resident population poor, helpless and despondent." The Commission concluded,

> The question is whether this vast wealth shall belong to persons who live here and who are permanently identified with the future of West Virginia, or whether it shall pass into the hands of persons who do not live here and who care nothing for our State except to pocket the treasures which lie buried in our hills.

The warning of the tax commission went unheeded.

Faced with the grim realities of our industrialized past, many readers wince at these painful images of dubious stereotypes of "radicals" and union organizers at war with state militias and the National Guard. And now, with the Lynns' remarkable documentary work at Whipple, a whole new sense about the victimization of women has come to light. So why should we mine the under-belly of West Virginia's agonizing past for these devilish details? Aren't some things better forgotten? Can't we just let bygones be bygones?

For more clarity on these issues I turned again to Lon Savage in *The Goldenseal Book of the West Virginia Mine Wars*, in an anniversary speech he gave at Matewan, West Virginia, on May 19, 1989:

> Let's tell everyone our history; let's brag about it; let's revel in it. Acknowledging and telling our history may even change the way we see ourselves. If the history of violence in Appalachian mining is ever to change, it will happen with an acknowl-edgement, a full airing, and an understanding of that history. . . . Most importantly it will help us understand ourselves . . . more rapidly than almost anything else we can do. (p. 48)

Epilogue

To wrap up the loose ends of this complex story, Michael Kline and I visited the Whipple Store again in late May of 2011 to touch base with Joy and Chuck Lynn. They told us that three days earlier, a man in his early nineties had visited the store. They showed him around the imposing porch, which he had known from his childhood. When they stepped inside the freight room, the man poked Joy on the shoulder, said, "Hey lady, did you ever hear of Esau? They got my mother with that Esau."

—Wess Harris

Truth Buried

Goldenseal

Goldenseal — West Virginia Traditional Life

February 10, 2011

Michael Kline
114 Boundary Avenue
Elkins, WV 26241

Dear Michael,

Thank you for your recent manuscript concerning the Whipple Store. I found it to be very interesting, though very challenging in certain respects. As we had discussed on the phone, our normal maximum manuscript length falls somewhere around 3,000 words. We are about double that here, I would estimate. Much of the wide-ranging industrial history in this manuscript could possibly be trimmed in favor of some additional specific details about the Whipple community and Whipple Colliery. But there are other, larger problems.

The main challenge we face from a publishing standpoint is the overall intent of this manuscript to expose the sins of the coal industry, accusing them of rape and murder on a grand scale. I'm not sure GOLDENSEAL is the right outlet for this sort of exposé. I don't take issue with or doubt the testimony of Joy and Chuck Lynn or their informants. As we discussed on the phone, I am even willing to address these sensitive issues in a special sidebar associated with a general history of the Whipple Store. The current manuscript, however, is very pointed in its intention and shows no quarter, not just with Whipple, but with the coal industry as a whole and with other capitalistic interests.

The history of West Virginia is painful at times, to be sure, and I don't shrink from my responsibility to address the tough parts in GOLDENSEAL as the occasion demands. Michael, I'm afraid this manuscript is simply beyond the pale when it comes to controversy. We cannot go to press with these industry-wide accusations of heinous behavior, especially without corroborating evidence or documentation.

I know you have put a lot of work into this story and have been anxious for a more positive response from me. I have read this story over twice, however, and don't see how it would fit in our pages. In the unlikely event that you would like to rework this story into something less provocative, I would be glad to help you in any way I can. Just let me know. In the meantime, I am returning your materials to you, with my regrets.

Sincerely,

John Lilly
Editor

JL:ca

Enclosures

West Virginia Division of Culture and History
The Cultural Center, 1900 Kanawha Boulevard East, Charleston, WV 25305-0300
304/558-0220   TDD 304/558-3562   FAX 304/558-2779

Behind the Coal Curtain
Efforts to Publish the Esau Story in West Virginia
Michael Kline

Michael Kline is an independent folklorist and audio producer in Elkins, West Virginia.

I WAS TIPPED OFF ABOUT THE WHIPPLE STORE BY MY FRIEND Wess Harris. For the past forty years I have been following local recollections of the early days of Union organizing through the coalfields of West Virginia and eastern Kentucky. With Carrie Kline, I have been a lifelong collector and singer of coal mining songs. I published an article about former United Mine Workers President Arnold Miller's memories growing up on Cabin Creek in the 1930s and '40s in *The Goldenseal Book of the West Virginia Mine Wars*, published by the West Virginia Division of Culture and History in 1991. Carrie Kline and I were asked by the Park Service Headquarters at Glen Jean to provide training in oral history gathering for their staff as they undertook a study of African-American mining culture and history in the New River Gorge. I have come at half a century of research in West Virginia by way of oral sources and have recorded hundreds of reflections and recollections of more than two generations of working people here.

West Virginia's official social history, especially as interpreted by the state's Division of Culture and History in Charleston, has never entertained the possibility of Esau. Mainstream historians, including those specializing in labor history have never touched it, though it is a documented undercurrent of coalfield lore and memories borne by some of our oldest neighbors and family members. Joy and Chuck Lynn, owners of the Whipple Company

Store, have not published or publicized the story of Esau widely out of a respect for the emotions still raw among decedents of those involved in the system. They agreed to my article with some reservations and I hope these concerns have been honored.

I initially wrote "Esau" for *Goldenseal* magazine, a folk life quarterly published by West Virginia's Division of Culture and History in Charleston. I have published a score of articles in *Goldenseal* over the past thirty-three years, and was anxious to reach those readers with this story. Through the development of the piece last fall and into the winter, I was in phone contact with the editor, John Lilly, an old friend of mine, about the emerging details, especially regarding Esau. I wanted him to know what was coming. And though he expressed nervousness about this revelation, nonetheless he encouraged me to finish and submit the manuscript by February 1. Sadly, he rejected my submission, because, as he explained, the piece "shows no quarter, not just with Whipple, but with the coal industry as a whole and with other capitalistic interests." I have since wondered when the coal industry became such a fragile flower that it should be somehow removed from scrutiny increasingly focused upon its dark and draconian past. I bet Mother Jones would have had some choice words for John Lilly. The air would have been blue.

Lilly's rejection letter is evidence of the sinister power of the coal industry then—and now—and its ability to intimidate well-meaning public service workers such as John Lilly, along with judges, state legislators, and anyone else who is in a position to protect the industry's image.

I sense the long shadow of Commissioner Randall Reid-Smith cast across the decision to suppress the Esau story. Reid-Smith has already made his coal industry loyalties abundantly clear. He serves at the will and pleasure of the governor.

The Lilly letter reminds me of that stifling feeling I first knew working in the coalfields as a community organizer in Johnson's War on Poverty in the mid-1960s. It was a sense of the isolation in which we were trying to generate programs for social change. We felt that nobody out there in mainstream USA, especially the bureaucrats writing Poverty War legislation and programs, could possibly have the slightest idea of challenges facing coalfield communities. In places where we worked there was a poverty of information coming in and going out, as though we had been left for dead. It was like a big brattice had been hung to shade out any light of understanding connecting us with the diverse social landscapes and economies defining much of the rest of the nation.

I remembered talk I heard as a child growing up in the Cold War era about human rights abuses in the Soviet Union. When the high-ranking leaders of the Communist Party during much of the twentieth century gained totalitarian control over the Russian people through stern measures to isolate them from other nations and ideas, we talked about human suffering going on "behind the Iron Curtain." It was a place, our leaders said, where ordinary people lived in fear and darkness.

As I discovered working for community self-determination in the coalfields of the 1960s, the political leadership of our state had woven for us, from the time of our coal mining ancestors, a Coal Curtain, a mantle of darkness and devaluation. The rest of the world has very little idea about the symbiotic relationship among the coal industry, the courts, and the hallways of state government in Charleston. Coal barons taught us to be suspicious of outsiders from the days of the earliest Union organizing efforts. They did not hesitate to label those entering the camps sans invitation as socialists, troublemakers, Reds! Ironically, we also learned to suspect outsiders through our experience with the coal barons—all too often outsiders who thought only of gain they might take from here back to there.

Isolation from the outside world and a fear of strangers: that's a mix which has all too often left us poor, destitute, and robbed of our natural birthright, that is, our water, air, natural landscapes, and the mineral wealth that lies beneath them. These treasures are ours, in common, by any fair standard of justice and democratic living and sharing. The blackout on news and censorship of historical truths behind this Coal Curtain today render us who live here confused and largely powerless. A recently composed song echoes the refrain:

> *Well tell me now who is to blame,*
> *who shakes King Coal's hand?*
> *Who fails to protect us,*
> *and who sells out our land?*
> *It's the greedy politicians*
> *at the company's beck and call,*
> *From the judges up to the president,*
> *I would blame them all*
> —Magpie (Greg Artzner & Terry Leonino), "Barons of King Coal"

Living in this climate of supreme corporate control and influence peddling, I feel this censorship keenly. We need to revitalize our labor history resources, not just here in West Virginia but all over the coalfields, as initiatives to strip us of our hard-fought labor rights are gaining momentum. We need to teach younger workers what is at stake in keeping a tight grasp on our common history. Tune in to freedom movements springing up all over the globe in places where the authorities said it could never happen. They are great sources of inspiration. Everyone seems ready to throw off the yoke.

Saturday
Gazette-Mail
FEBRUARY 25, 2012   CHARLESTON, WEST VIRGINIA

Smiles

To history buff Michael Kline of Elkins, who won a Plattner Award for Creative Nonfiction for his account of coal industry oppression once centered at the Whipple company store in Fayette County — and also won a state History Hero award with his wife.

Photo credit: Lewis Wickes Hine, National Archives.

When he took the above photograph in 1908, Lewis Hine noted, "Vance, a Trapper Boy, 15 years old. Has trapped for several years in a West Va. Coal mine. $.75 a day for 10 hours work."

Scratching the Surface

Wess Harris

PUBLICATION IN 2011 OF MICHAEL KLINE'S RESEARCH ON THE Esau system of forced sexual servitude in the coalfields of West Virginia was a gamble. Documentation was limited. The opportunity to gather additional primary source documentation was rapidly growing to a close—potential sources were dying off. If we were unable to further document the Esau system, going public would result in very legitimate criticism that the system may never have existed. The story was published in the hope that established scholars would become interested and would lend a hand with much-needed and time-sensitive research on the topic.

Kline's Summer 2011 article in *Appalachian Heritage* earned a Plattner Award and the wrath of wider academia. Professors demanded more sources and more concrete proof, but none stepped forward to assist with the work that arguably should have been done decades earlier by those very scholars. The work of further documenting the existence of Esau scrip fell to a very limited number of unfunded independent scholars.

We now have additional documentation based on hundreds of in-person interviews, followed when possible by phone conversations and e-mails. None of the sources were familiar with Kline's work and none were prompted beyond a simple query: Have you ever heard of Esau? Names and addresses have been redacted to protect rape victims and their families. Legitimate researchers known to have a high level of integrity and willing to sign a confidentiality agreement will be permitted to view a source list.

Spring 2009, Fayette County, West Virginia, a middle-aged professional woman reports, "My grandmother took the Esau"

and "My mother does not know" about the grandmother's participation. She confirmed the sexual nature of the transaction and
elaborated on the system.

September 18, 2010, Summersville, West Virginia,
_____ of Huntington, West Virginia, reported hearing of "super scrip" in the lumber camps of Marlinton. It was for women
only and she never understood what it was—thinking it was a
computer script (font).

September 16, 2012, _____ , age 77, of Parkersburg, West
Virginia, stated he knew of Esau.

September 16, 2012, _____ of _____ Parkersburg,
sent an e-mail which read in part, "Today in Parkersburg at the
Harvest Moon Festival I met a gentleman selling the two books. . . .
I was born and raised in a coal camp area outside of Beckley and
was surprised when I moved here the lack of knowledge of such
life elsewhere in the SAME state." On September 18, that same individual e-mails further: "I have in fact heard of Esau . . . and not
the biblical aspect. Just one of the many unknown burdens and
strife of the early miners. I was in my late teens when I finally had
it explained to me by my mother's oldest brother who worked in
the mines all his life." A third e-mail, September 20, offers, "In re-
gards to the Esau matter . . . Three uncles on my mother's side of
the family were all deep shaft miners. Two worked in the Sophia,
Coal City, Welch area. Both worked for the same mines each
time retiring from them. One worked for a mine around Oak
Hill Glen Jean area. My father and grandfather were both carpen-
ters working for the Large Blue Jay/Ritter Lumber Company in
Beaver building company houses for both the area mines and the
lumber company who also had their camps. Esau was much like
the cousin no one wanted to admit they had. . . . It was there . . . it
was real . . . you just didn't talk about it."

Early October 2012, an unnamed neighbor of Michael Kline,
Elkins, West Virginia, at the Forest Festival knew of Esau in

Webster, Upshur, and Pocahontas counties and noted that women also knew of birth control/unwanted pregnancy "remedies." "Just what you had to do to survive."

November 2012, _____ , a very elderly man at the Capital City Art and Craft Fair wrote, "I learned about Esau from my grandparents."

December 10, 2012, _____ , professional staff person at a Beckley, West Virginia, nursing home shared stories of Esau heard from patients. Also provided personal family history from northern West Virginia. A lengthy interview was conducted and recorded at the nursing facility.

July 20, 2013, an e-mail from _____ , college-educated native of southern West Virginia currently living in Ohio states, "When miners had big debts at the company store, the bosses would offer them overtime if they could go to the guy's house and have sex with his wife and daughters. Many a miner raised kids they didn't father. If a man was fired for missing work due to being drunk, the wife would go to the mine and have sex with the mine boss or bosses to get her husband's job back."

October 11, 2013, at Tamarack in Beckley, _____ of _____ Elkton, Virginia, by telephone and e-mail stated knowledge of Esau and volunteered that it was "absolutely true."

October 22, 2013, _____ of Charleston said that her mother's grandmother "took Esau" and that her husband's father knew of Esau as a scrip.

November 24, 2013, _____ at the Capital City Art and Craft Fair in Charleston, _____ said that her mother knew of the Esau system.

December 21, 2013, at the Purple Onion in the Town Center Mall in Charleston, West Virginia, a woman would not give her name but said she grew up in Holden, knew what went on, and had heard rumors as a child. She said folks bragged that it was "not in Holden."

July 3, 2014, _____ of Ravenswood, grew up in Creston, West Virginia, in Calhoun County. She knew of Esau from when growing up.

August 23, 2014, _____ of near Beckley said his grand-mother, who died at the age of 101, had mentioned "what she had to do to keep food on the table." He later left a phone message to the author saying, "I believe Esau was prevalent throughout the entire part of southern West Virginia."

August 30, 2014, at Jackson's Mill near Weston, West Virginia, _____ reported that her ninety-eight-year-old grandmother told her of Esau.

October 26, 2014, in an interview and written note, _____ at Mountaineer Week in Morgantown offered, "Heard about Esau from old miners in community I grew up with . . . women had to do favors for the super . . ."

May 13, 2015, _____ , a young professional woman employed with _____ reported that while growing up she heard her grandmother from McDowell County speak of "Esau scrip." She did not know the meaning of the term until recently.

October 20, 2015, an unnamed woman from Beckley engaged in conversation at a book signing at Taylor Books in Charleston. She learned of Esau from her grandfather, but it was "not some-thing you talked about outside the family."

October 24, 2015, a well-dressed woman at the book festival in Charleston made the following comments: "My grandfather was mine foreman. I saw Esau as a kid. Grandma knew of it and had some—I saw it. Of course, Grandma did not use the Esau. Grandpa was mine foreman."

November 21, 2015, at the Capitol City Art and Craft Show in Charleston, _____ spoke of spending thirty-five years in the mines. He knew of Esau from his grandfather. He was from Mingo County (first Esau source from Mingo).

November 31, 2015, at the Mountaineer Week Craft Show in Morgantown two women from Wyoming County (perhaps in their late fifties, at least one a teacher) were queried about Esau. Both remembered hearing the term Esau but forgot what it was. When I told the story from Whipple amidst a crowd of shoppers, I noticed one of the women in tears and much distress. Not wanting to cause emotional trauma, I ended the tale and gently commented, "You knew what that was, didn't you?" Both responded, "Yes, that is what we heard as children." I thanked them for sharing and apologized for any emotional stress invoked. I told them how important it was and that to date we had no sources on Esau from Wyoming County. Both virtually in unison said, "We grew up in Beaver." Beaver is near Beckley and in the region where other Esau stories have surfaced.

We ended the conversation, and later in the afternoon I was able to give them a complimentary copy of *Truth Be Told,* first edition. Perhaps knowing they are not alone will be of some help.

Photo credit: Lewis Wickes Hine, National Archives.

Eleven-year-old "tipple boy," Turkey Knob Mine, MacDonald, West Virginia, 1908.

The Rented Girl
A Closer Look at Women in the Coalfields
Michael Kline

THIS CHAPTER FURTHER EXPLORES THE RELATIONSHIP OF KING Coal to women in West Virginia since we became an extractive state a century and a half ago. I recently revisited an interview recorded twenty years ago in Wheeling, West Virginia. The seventy-year-old man at the live end of the microphone told me he was raised across the Ohio River near Lansing, Ohio, and grew up in a "Polish patch" in the shadow of a large tipple. He said:

> Most of the stories from my dad's generation were of abuse by the coal companies, you know, getting the shaft, from how they weighed the coal to charging you with digging dirty coal. And if you got three dirty coals you were fired. Or if you had occasion to stand up to one of the bosses like a lot of those people did—my dad was a feisty one and never allowed anyone to spit in his soup, as we always say—you were fired. And either you had to go beg for your job back, or if you were married, your wife would have to go sometime and beg for your job behind closed doors in an office. Now I couldn't prove it, but that's what my mother said. And what went on behind those closed doors, my mother wouldn't say. She was too much of a lady. But at that time we were old enough to realize what could have been going on just so a man could get his job back.

It suddenly occurred to me that I had never before looked critically at coal camp women's experiences. Nor had I ever read accounts of ways in which women were affected by coal company policies, except that they were often poor and hungry, especially in times of labor unrest. In the face of such vivid memories as I heard in Wheeling, where would I turn for an unraveling of these issues?

Why have these women's issues not been addressed by our regional historians, public museums, and institutions of higher learning? What about these troubling references we're hearing in oral testimonials now surfacing in our coal mining communities? Where are the written accounts to parallel the spoken references to this sexual servitude? If such predatory practices were carried out in plain view in "wide-open" industrial centers like Wheeling, what about more isolated settings? What about labor camps so far back in the mountains that they were accessible only by rail and served only by a company store—places you couldn't walk away from?

Since the publication of my article "Esau in the Coalfields" in the Summer 2011 edition of *Appalachian Heritage*, and later in *Dead Ringers* (2012), numerous accounts of institutionalized forced sexual servitude in the coalfields have surfaced. Perhaps the most compelling came from an activities director at a nursing home in southern West Virginia. She is in her late forties. After reading of Esau in *Dead Ringers*, she approached editor Wess Harris saying she had heard similar stories of sexual exploitation from a few of her older residents.

Some weeks later, as Harris, Carrie Kline, and I visited the nursing home, the activities director unexpectedly shared her own family story quite apart from those she had heard from her older clients. She agreed on the spot to record and go public with it.

All my people are from [a small city in northern] West Virginia. To start the story, my maternal great-grandmother

Loretta, at a very young age was sold to one of the coal companies outside of town. Maybe she was rented was more the word, 'cause we have a [lease] agreement from one of the coal companies for her. The family story is that [company agents] came into town that day and it was fifteen to twenty girls that they took to the coal camps. And she was twelve years old the first time she went. And they would keep them up there for anywhere between four to six months at a time. And if the girls had babies, the babies would be taken and sold. And this would have been in the [nineteen]-twenties.

I understand what Loretta did, because I know what it's like to be a twelve-year-old girl from the coalfields of West Virginia. I am not like her, but she's my blood and I still love her. So I'm very protective over her memory, even though maybe I shouldn't be. So it's kind of hard for me to share this story with you because I'm still very guarded by it. I don't want people to judge her because of what she did. I mean, I think it's important that the story gets out, but yet, I don't want people to go, "Oh, my God! She's a horrible woman." Because she did what she had to do. Because she didn't have any other choice.

The families would sign the girls up to go to the coal camps. It was a pretty common practice. It was just so far back in the mountains that they would be in there for months. The only way in was the railroad. So they would take the train in and then they would take the train back. But there was no town; it wasn't like a town, 'cause they were so far back in the mountains. So they would just live there. And the girls would stay and they would be comfort girls. They would call them comfort girls, or comfort wives, or coal wives. I mean it was just such a common practice that it wasn't unusual. And the [company agents] never took older women. They were always the younger girls.

I guess they weren't needed at home, or they had too many at home. I think Loretta went because there was just so many in her family. There was just lots and lots of kids [to feed] in that family. And some people said Loretta was just so wild, she wanted to go. There was quite a few girls that didn't want to go. That was like the big threat, you know, [that parents used with unruly daughters], "If you don't straighten up, I'll put you on the train to the camp." And there was quite a few young girls that the parents would put a sack over their heads and put them on the train to the camp. And it would run right out of town straight to the camp.

It's such a common story it's kind of funny that you guys haven't heard of it. Maybe it's just a northern West Virginia thing. The mountains are just so rugged. There aren't roads. There was no place to go if you got loose. I mean you're so far in the woods that no one tried to run, 'cause where were you going to go? But a lot of the girls didn't mind being there. Life was so hard at home that you did your time and—

They were fed, and that's what was expected [in return], to be comfort girls in the camp. That's how they lived their life, you know. That's who they were. But I do remember that there was talk of an orphanage in Tennessee. And as Loretta got older—too old to be a comfort girl any longer—[the baby selling was] what she handled. Her job was to take the babies to Tennessee. I imagine Loretta was making a lot of money with the babies, because she didn't have any qualms about selling her own babies in Tennessee. She would show up at the orphanage and they'd say, "Where did you get the baby?"

And she'd go, "It's mine." It wouldn't be hers. But that's what she'd put on the birth certificate. And she had to have been in with the people that was running the coal camp.

I mean if you think about it, how could you survive at that time? I mean if you're a woman and the only thing you have to make money with is your body, and you end up pregnant, you can't afford to feed that baby. So what are you going to do?

And there's my great-grandmother standing there going, "Well, I'll buy the baby so you can get back to work," and you're fifteen years old. And a lot of the girls are going to go, "Okay. Here's the baby. I need to get back to work." And then Loretta gives the young girl, you know, fifty bucks. The young girl gets money, I mean, I don't know what she was selling them for. I just know that's what she did. So then she got however many more waiting down the line. I mean, it just, I don't know, it just—. People like Loretta have to be related to somebody. And unfortunately she's related to me. You know, it's just—(laughs). You know when you hear it out loud, it's like, "Oh my God. That's what my great-grandmother did!"

When you share your story it's a powerful thing, because she doesn't only belong to me now. Now she belongs to you guys [too] because I've told you about her. And all these years she was just mine. It makes you wonder though, was it the guys who came in and bought the young women for the coal camps, were they the terrible people? Or was it her family that encouraged her to go to the coal camps?

There are lots of people I grew up with. That's what happened to their grandmothers. It's not an unusual story in that town.

The activities director followed this vivid family recollection with a professional one.

> I'm an activities director at this nursing home and we've got one lady that talks about the Esau story. She talked about getting a new pair of shoes. And she didn't have enough money to pay for the shoes. It was at the Whipple Store. And one of the guys at the store said, "Well, I can get you a pair of shoes."
>
> Another woman in the store pulled on her dress, and she says, "You don't want to go upstairs."
>
> "Yeah I do, there's a pair of shoes up there he's going to show me."
>
> And the woman says again, "You don't want to go and see those shoes." And she kept trying to tell her, you know, "You don't want those shoes."
>
> "Well I need a new pair of shoes." And she's looking down at her feet, "And the kids need shoes." And the other woman's shaking her head. So finally the lady went up and got her shoes. So she came back downstairs and she had all these shoes. And everyone had gotten real quiet while she's telling me this story. "Well I went up and got my shoes," she said finally. And then she got real quiet. And then the other ladies kind of had their heads down and they didn't say anything for a while. And of course I'm not from around here, so I didn't get the story at first.
>
> So I'm sitting there and looking at her and they all got real quiet. And I'm like, "Well, what about the shoes?" And I mean it was dead silence. And I'm thinking, what's going on? So she started crying and I put my arm around her and I said, "Honey, what about the shoes?"
>
> And she looked over at me and she says, "You don't know what it cost for those shoes."

And I says, "What do you mean?" And then another woman started crying. And I looked at her and I says, "Okay, what are you guys talking about?"

So then another woman scooted up next to me and she says, "When your kids need shoes, there's things you do upstairs in that room, and if you really need shoes," she says, "that's what you have to do to get them."

And then another lady says, "It's like Esau."

And I looked at her and I said, "What are you talking about?" I had never heard the whole Esau story, and then they explained to me the concept of Esau where, if you have someone in your family that can't work, then you can take a chit out and pay with your body to get another day's pay or another week's worth of groceries, or whatever. And that woman that said she needed four pairs of shoes, she just kind of cried and put her head down, and you should have seen the look on those women's faces. I mean, they was pure white, and they just put their head down and—I mean, they knew exactly what she was talking about. And of course I was dense. I didn't get it at first.

Esau is a strange term for me because I came from a background where the women weren't often married. To be a married woman and have children at home and have to go through that could be even more horrible. But it's interesting to see the reaction of these women after all these years—they're in their eighties. And it was just like they were living it all over again. Like someone brought something horrible up and it happened to them again.

As for my own family, I've got one aunt that says that [my great-grandmother] Loretta, was strong and survived, where other women, you know, they crawled under a rock and let some man beat them and they were victims. And [according to my aunt] Loretta wasn't a victim. She was strong and she took charge of her life and I should be proud of her because she wasn't a victim. It's a different way to look at it, you know? So I should be proud of her? Who knows? (Laughs) It's whatever helps you sleep at night.

"Whether a woman is raped at gunpoint or trafficked into sexual slavery by an occupying force, the sexual abuse will shape not just her own but her community's future for years to come.

"Survivors face emotional torment, psychological damage, physical injuries, disease, social ostracism and many other consequences that can devastate their lives."

—Amnesty International

Photo credit: Tony Oppegard.

Some may Lay on A Hill of Green
Or under a mountain to not be seen
Dust Filled Lungs That never mend
Grandpa, Dad or Dear Old Friend

Most Are gone, Their Journey Through
This Breed of men Are now so Few
The Flames Are out on Carbide Lamps
Only memories Left of Old Coal Camps

James D. Kilgore

The Memo

Larry Layne as told to Michael and Carrie Kline

THE PUBLICATION OF "ESAU IN THE COALFIELDS" HAS LED TO connections with many other coal industry atrocities against working West Virginia families, beyond the upstairs curtained room at the Whipple Company Store. At eighty-one years of age, Lawrence Layne looks back on his career as a federal mine inspector in West Virginia, and later in Alabama, where he is now retired with his wife Sue.

Carrie Kline and I visited the Laynes at their home in the Birmingham area on February 14, 2015, and recorded their recollections sitting around the dining room table.

Layne is easily one of the most knowledgeable, available sources about the whole arena of coal mining, from the hand-loading days of his youth to the fully mechanized industry of today. He is all too familiar with how safety challenges and practices are overshadowed by pressures for maximum production and profit from distant corporate offices. His compelling commentary of the culture of mining inspection at a time of rapid corporate expansion throughout the industry makes the blood run cold. What follows are verbatim excerpts from the interview. His story begins in the cradle of industrial tragedy with memories of a mining explosion that took over five hundred lives, including those of his grandfather and uncle.

Larry Layne: I was born at Monongah, West Virginia, and raised in Harrison County, those small mining communities. Went to grade school in a little place called McWhorter, went to Lost Creek Middle School, and then to Shinnston High School. Monongah is where they had the big explosion in 1907. My grandfather on my mother's side was killed in that explosion. And my dad was ten years old when his oldest brother, sixteen years old, was killed in that explosion also.

And I grew up mainly doing farm work. My dad and his friend were mine foreman and superintendent at a large mine, and they just started this small mine on their own. So between high school in the summers I worked—I wasn't eighteen, but I worked at the mine for my dad. And my dad would come in the morning and make the preshift examination. And I had about six hand-loaders and one horse driver. So during the day, everything depended on me. I checked the men out, checked the men in, got their powder and their caps, and kept track of everything. Ordered all supplies and so forth. I did all this before I was eighteen. So I became very interested in the coal mining business, and I have gone from the hand-loading into all phases of coal mining—mechanical, continuous miners, longwall. I've been in coal mining over forty some years, so anything you want to know about coal mining, I can tell you.

Well, as soon as I turned twenty-five, I took the mine foreman's examination and became a certified mine foreman and preshift examiner. So, up until I was twenty-five, I [was a rank-and-file union coal miner], and I worked at Humphrey No. 7, Christopher Coal Company, in Morgantown.

In the mine I learned to do everything. I was a machine operator. I could operate the continuous miner, cutting machines, loading machines, shuttle cars, shot fireman. I did every job that ever came open because I wanted to learn everything. Later I left the union and went into management and started my career there, which was section boss, shift foreman, mine foreman, superintendent, general superintendent, and eventually manager of mines.

After I left coal mining management, I went with the Federal Bureau of Mines. And while working for the Bureau of Mines, I went to many, many mine fires and many explosions in northern

West Virginia. If you go back several years, at one time or another every big mine up there had an explosion or a fire in it, and so I worked all of those explosions and fires. And today I think I've got more experience in mine fires and explosion work, and rescue and recovery, than anybody in the United States.

Michael Kline: Well, I was going to say.

LL: So I worked as an inspector for five years, and then I was promoted to supervisor. I went to Wheeling, West Virginia. And then they passed the 1969 Health and Safety Act, and that required four inspections a year at each underground mine, plus spot inspections every week at real gassy mines, plus two inspections a year for surface mines. And they couldn't get any inspectors with that test they were giving. So they had to eliminate the test, and they just started hiring them through application. So we got some doozies. They gave me fifteen new ones at Wheeling to train. Out of the fifteen, I had about four good ones, and the rest of them, they didn't have the knowledge. You can go to a coal mine and work for twenty years if you're on one section doing one thing. But a coal mine inspector should be at least a mine foreman who knows the entire mine, knows how to ventilate the mine, knows how to manage roof control. And they just didn't have those men. And that's what happened, that they had to bring in people that were really not qualified, and they didn't have the experience. And so they hired—I think they had 1,400—brought in 1,400 new men. So we just didn't have the proper personnel to inspect the mines, but we did the best we could.

Because of his vast experience Layne was called in to inspect No. 9 when it was reopened in September of 1970. Two years earlier he had arrived at the disaster scene only two and a half hours after the initial explosion, which further qualified him to lead this inspection.

LL: Consol No. 9 blew up on November the 20th, 1968. That's when seventy-eight men were killed and sealed in the mine. Are you familiar with that incident? Okay. So, of course, I worked a little bit there. We had to seal it. And then I went to Washington, DC, helped write the '69 Act [on Coal Mine Health and Safety, inspired by the No. 9 disaster].

When I came back to Morgantown, they had so many complaints from the union there about inspectors being lax and not doing their jobs. So they sent me from Morgantown to Fairmont, and I started inspecting the mines. That's where Consol No. 9 is located, in the Fairmont area. I had a difficult time with Mountaineer Coal Company [a Consol subsidiary], which owned No. 9, because they were very, very belligerent. Mountaineer Coal Company officials thought the new Act was not for them—the new law was not for them.

MK: In what sense?

LL: They wanted to do everything the way they had always done it—their methods and their policies and so forth. They did not want to comply with the Federal Coal Mine Health and Safety Act of '69. And because of the lack of—due lack of diligence, that's what happened at No. 9 that caused it to blow up.

After a series of repeated explosions in the week following November 20, 1968, No. 9 was sealed with the bodies of seventy-eight coal miners inside. Almost two years later, in September of 1970, Consol and its subsidiary Mountaineer Coal reopened No. 9 to begin retrieving the bodies, launch an investigation into the causes of the disaster, and fire up renewed production. Layne was on hand as a federal inspector at the time and soon uncovered disturbing evidence of what sounded like criminal negligence from a source he felt he could trust. This revelation, coupled with his own discovery twenty-two months earlier of a broken glass case and missing Mod's Run fan charts just two hours after the explosion, began to smell like a mixture of foul play and cover-up.

LL: And while I was at No. 9, I found a man who was an electrician, and on this shift I was outside in charge taking care of the phone calls and notes and everything. And I saw this man I recognized because I had seen him in Fairmont. That's where I lived at the time. And so I got to talking to him, and he was an outside electrician. We were talking about the explosion, and I asked him about the Mod's Run fan, when it went down, and why nobody knew about it. Because each fan has to have an alarm system, and that alarm has to be stationed where somebody can see it at all times. And he said, "Well, that alarm has been disconnected." And I said, "Who disconnected it?" He said, "Me and the chief electrician." I said, "Why did you do that?" And he said, "The chief electrician said that that fan kept going down, and they were having trouble with it. And every time the fan went down, they didn't want to pull the men out of the mine." So this man told me, he said, "The chief electrician said they told him to disconnect the fan alarm system." He said, "So we disconnected the fan alarm system."

MK: *They* told him, meaning—?

LL: He said "they," meaning upper management. That would be your superintendent or mine foreman. *They* told the chief electrician, told him to disconnect [the fan alarm system]. And so I wrote a memorandum, and I told exactly what he said, that he had disconnected the fan alarm system. And when the fan stopped, the men were supposed to be withdrawn within fifteen minutes. Okay, they disconnected this fan alarm system, so when that fan went down, [the alarm didn't sound and] they didn't withdraw the men. They just let them stay in the mine. They had three other fans, but each fan has a certain area to ventilate. So this area the Mod's Run fan [was supposed to have been ventilating] wasn't ventilated. And that's what happened. It let the gas build up, and then something exploded. Some ignition caused the explosion.

So I wrote that memorandum, and I sent it to my district manager, Jim Michael. And, of course, the district manager read it, and he gave it to my immediate supervisor, Joe Marcelli, and Joe signed it. And then quite a few days later it was sent to Mount Hope to Bill Park, who was the district manager over all of West Virginia. And Bill Park wrote on there to his secretary and said, "Deposit this with the other No. 9 information." I asked about that memo, and the only answer I could get was, "I sent it on." My boss said, "I sent it on up the ladder." And I never heard anything more about it until forty years later; Bonnie Stewart in her research was going through the archives, and she said in the bottom of a box she found my memo. So she used my memo and came down here and spent a lot of time with me (laughs), and I helped her write the book.

Bonnie Stewart, PhD, came to West Virginia a decade ago to teach journalism at West Virginia University in Morgantown. She soon developed an interest in No. 9 and began researching the meager paper trail of information about the causes of the explosion. In 2008, Stewart came across Layne's 1970 memorandum which put a whole new spin on a case which had never even come to trial. In 2012, her stellar investigative study, No. 9, *was published by West Virginia University Press. Her book is a total rewrite of West Virginia's industrial history, revealing the precise nature of ongoing atrocities by coal bosses and the regulatory culture in which this criminal negligence has been largely ignored by state and federal regulators. Most of the mine inspection force has been looking the other way since the beginning of the industry a century and a half ago. The travesty of our political leaders facing TV cameras against a backdrop of billowing smoke and flame, calling these corporate crimes "Acts of God," is sickeningly familiar to coalfield residents.*

LL: I was at another [nearby] mine, but when I heard about the explosion at No. 9 I went over [to the disaster scene] and started checking the fans to see what was running. When I went to Mod's Run, it's somewhere around eight o'clock [two and a half hours after the explosion]. At each fan there is an enclosed metal box with a glass front on it that has a pressure recording gauge in it. And that box is locked. Someone had broken the glass [at the Mod's Run fan] and taken all of the pressure recording gauges out. These are like charts, pressure recording charts, that will tell you when the fan stopped. Someone had taken them out.

And I asked my boss, "Who took the recording gauges?" He said, "The state has them." So I went to John Ashcroft—John was the senior state inspector—and John said, "No, I don't have them." He said, "Your people have them." I said, "No, my people don't have them." I said, "Joe Marcelli said you have them."

Well, that was the end of it. Nobody ever mentioned—in the [three-hour] hearing they had at Fairmont, nobody ever mentioned who broke that box open and took those recording gauges. Nobody ever mentioned it. And I couldn't—it was just hard for me to believe [reading the transcripts from the one and only hearing in Fairmont] that the top mining people in the state and the federal would let something like that go. And I just—I just couldn't hardly believe it. But anyway [the fan charts], like my memo, turned up about forty years later.

And I used to work with a guy named Jim Simon, and Jim lived within—he told me 200 yards of this Mod's Run fan. And Jim and I were real good friends, and he knew he could talk to me confidentially. And he said, "Larry," he said, "That fan has been down many, many, many times." He said, "I work midnight shift at JoAnn mine." and he said, "I sleep during the day, and that fan—those big fans are ten feet in diameter. And they make a high-pitch hum sound, and they'll put you right to sleep." And he said, "Every time that fan would stop, I'd wake up." And he said, "Many, many times that fan has been down for days at a time." He said, "I called the superintendent, Mr. Turner, at No. 9 and told him that the fan was down. And Mr. Turner said, 'We know it, but we don't need that fan.'" And Jim said, "That fan's been down many times." But that's why the alarm was disconnected, because after fifteen minutes, you're supposed to withdraw the men if a fan goes down. The mine blew up on November 20, 1968, on Wednesday morning at five o'clock.

MK: In the age of space exploration we couldn't make a fan that would run dependably?

LL: Well, most of them did, but they were having some kind of problems with this fan. What the problem was, I don't know. Somebody said the blades were out of balance. And when they get out of balance and they're turning at such high revolutions that the blades fly off. And some of the people living close to that fan said that morning they did hear that banging noise, so. But the terrible thing—that's why the mine—that's why we got seventy-eight men sealed in the mine. They worked from 1968 up to '78, recovering bodies for ten years. There's nineteen that they never recovered, and they're still in there. They're sealed in there.

MK: So the real truth of this story really has never come out?

LL: Oh, no. No. But Bonnie's done a good job of trying to bring it out. And they were supposed to continue those hearings, and they never did. Never did. And, like I said, I read the transcripts. Not one person mentioned the fan charts. Not one person asked a

question about who broke the box open and took the fan charts—
the people doing the questioning. They had the top bureau man
there, top state man there, and top company man there with their
attorneys, and nobody asked the question where the fan chart
was. And the fan charts will tell you everything. Tell you for the
past year how many times the fan went down.

MK: Were you asked to be a witness? Were inspectors called as
witnesses?

LL: No, no. No, no, unh-uh. Inspectors weren't called.

MK: And how long after that hearing was it before Consol settled
with the widows for $10,000?

LL: They settled with that $10,000 very rapidly. Very rapidly.
Because, you see, two weeks later my memo came out. And if
they'd had my memo about the fan being down and the alarm
being pulled and wired around, then they'd have had a whole new
case. But, as Bonnie says in the book, two weeks before my memo
was written, [most of the widows] settled for $10,000.

And now that my memo has come to surface, I've talked to
several attorneys. Three different organizations have called me.
And they said what they have to do—as one guy said, "I have to
find something to hang my hat on." He said they have to tell the
judge that new evidence has come up that was not available at the
time—my memo and Bonnie's book.

MK: Is there anything else that we should [talk about]?

LL: Well, I was telling you about this mine in Whitwell, Tennessee,
where those thirteen men got killed. The mine blew up in, seemed
like it was '82, and I made that investigation. I was subpoenaed by

Kennedy's subcommittee investigation. So I had to go down there and testify before the Senate. And, of course, I don't pull punches. I tell everything just exactly as it is. And those widows ended up getting a million dollars apiece. They sued the company and they got a million dollars apiece.

I was happy that they got a million dollars apiece—happy that I could do something to help them. And I hope the same is true for the relatives of No. 9.

The textbox below contains a transcript of Larry Layne's long buried memo. Because a recent FOIA request for Layne's memo was successful, a full-color image of his original handwritten memo is included on the following page.

James L. Michael
Sept. 15, 1970

On Sept. 5, 1970, 12 AM–8 AM shift, the Mod's Run substation was energized for the first time since the explosion of Nov. 20, 1968. The electrician (name withheld by request) reported that while reenergizing the substation he found evidence to indicate that the Femco fan alarm system for Mod's Run fan had been rendered inoperative before the explosion. The fan alarm system had been bridged with jumper wires; therefore when the fan would stop or slow down there was no way of anyone knowing about it because the alarm system was by-passed. This information was reported to me Sept. 15, 1970.

L.L. Layne

James S. M. Pol. — Sept 15, 1970

On Sept. 5, 1970, 0 am – 5 am shift, the Mods Run substation was energized for the first time since the explosion of Nov 20, 1968. The electrician (name withheld by request) reported that while reenergizing the substation he found evidence to indicate that the Framco fan alarm system for Mods Run fan had been rendered inoperable before the explosion. The fan alarm system had been bridged with jumper wires; therefore when the fan would stop or slow down, there was no way of anyone knowing about it because the alarm signal was bypassed. This information was reported to me Sept 15, 1970.

S. S. Layne

Copy to
W. R. Park.
Manshulek

Enter in Notes.

JM.
9/18/70

BUREAU OF MINES
MORGANTOWN, W.V.
SEP 18 1970

Journalist William C. Blizzard (pictured above) was proud into his ninth decade that as a youth he had achieved the rank of Eagle Scout. His father, Bill, had actively encouraged the Boy Scouts of America to become involved in the early coal camps. Official historians for the State of West Virginia persist in labeling Bill an "ardent socialist."

Photo courtesy of the Radford Archives, William C. Blizzard/When Miners March Collection.

Even heroes gotta fish. Bill Blizzard relaxes outside his home in Winfield, West Virginia.
Photo courtesy of the Radford Archives, William C. Blizzard/ When Miners March Collection.

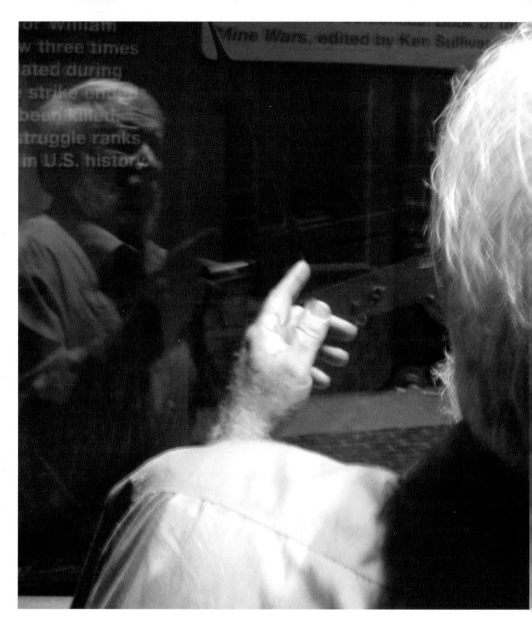

Reflections. Wess Harris has provided Truth Tours of the West Virginia State Museum to over 1,000 students and union members from around the country. Anti-miner bias, falsehoods, and design flaws are contrasted with the content of the When Miners March Traveling Museum, which he curates. Note that the reflection permits visitors to see themselves in the glass but renders a clear view of exhibits virtually impossible. Throughout the State Museum, overlapping audio ensures that visitors will be at little risk of understanding what is offered. See p.154 to glimpse state priorities. *Photo by Tom Rhule.*

William C. Blizzard, Wess Harris, and students from Xavier University share the picket line with miners from Local 8843.

Photo courtesy of the When Miners March Traveling Museum Collection.

Parked in the spot reserved for the commissioner of the West Virginia Division of Culture and History bearing Randall Reid-Smith's unique vanity plate, his vehicle also displays another passion. The Friends of Coal logo on his window is the registered trademark of the West Virginia Coal Owner's Association. *Photo by Wess Harris.*

Photo Credit: MSHA

Upper Big Branch rock-dusting machine pictured where it was found outside the mine. "When MSHA put power on the machine to test it as part of the investigation, the motor burned up."
Source: Industrial Homicide: Report on the Upper Big Branch Mine Disaster (UMWA, 2011), 52.

The well-rock-dusted mine cannot explode. Safe, legal mines are white, not black.
Photo by Wess Harris.

Cecil Roberts, president of the United Mine Workers of America.

Photo credit: Charleston Gazette.

West Virginia's Gilded History

Tom Rhule

Tom Rhule is an independent journalist, researcher, and blogger from Charleston, West Virginia. He has a reputation for finding stories that mainstream journalists have missed—or have chosen to avoid.

West Virginia's Golden Horseshoe Society is the longest running program of its kind in the United States. Since it began, more than 15,000 eighth graders have received the Golden Horseshoe Award in recognition of their knowledge of West Virginia history. Upon bestowing the accolade, the state ceremoniously inducts students as "knights" and "ladies" of the Golden Horseshoe Society.[1]

The West Virginia Department of Education promotes the "Society" to develop good citizenship in students.[2] A close examination of its origin reveals a concept of citizenship far removed from the democratic ideals of our nation.

In an interview about the State Historic Preservation Officer's willingness to sacrifice the historic resource at Blair Mountain to the mountaintop removal industry, Chris Green, professor at Marshall University, recently revealed, "I have students who were top-of-the-line Golden Horseshoe people who don't know about the mine wars."[3]

Responding to a congressionally mandated study over twenty years ago, ten prominent historians recommended Blair Mountain as a site worth preserving. Their reason was crystal clear: "West Virginia's labor history is part of a larger historical theme which illustrates the struggle for liberties promised in the Bill of Rights."[4]

West Virginia's mine wars erupted in 1912, then resumed in 1919 after World War I. During the mine wars state leaders, coal companies, and their local newspapers all portrayed the uprising as sedition, then later downplayed it all as little more than a series of wage disputes. Despite efforts by politically appointed state education leaders and mercenary revisionist historians to revise and minimize West Virginia's sordid history, there still remains enough evidence to prove that in 1921 the mine workers marched to battle for their civil liberties—for freedom of speech and assembly, freedom from the industrial feudalism of company towns, and freedom from the terrorism inflicted by the operators' private military.[5]

Simply stated, the Battle of Blair Mountain was an attempt by citizens to liberate the southern coalfields of West Virginia. Those who marched weren't the seditious rioters and bomb-throwing Bolsheviks they were being portrayed as at the time; they were patriots bent on redeeming their state from a rule of terror.[6]

Although the West Virginia Department of Education's official Golden Horseshoe Society website describes the program's originator as a noted historian, the state agency fails to do Phil Conley justice. Before starting the Golden Horseshoe Society, Conley was the human relations officer for the Consolidated Coal Company, running a blurb sheet for a coalition of coal owners that tagged themselves the West Virginia Publicity Commission. In 1921, Conley became first managing director for the American Constitutional Association (ACA), an organization so close to the West Virginia Department of Education that by May of '21 the two agencies literally shared the same office space.[7]

In *When Miners March*, author William C. Blizzard recognized the ACA as a pro-fascist outfit, further revealing that "in order to secure a 'good press' and . . . to continue a tight grip over governmental affairs in the Mountain State, a group of operators and public officials . . . hand in glove . . . banded together to form the American Constitutional Association."[8]

Conley is on record as having told the Executive Committee of the ACA that its partnership with state schools would enable the organization to "reach the adults through the medium of the children." Conley also reported to his group that the ACA had the potential of influencing eleven thousand teachers, and then proceeded to do so directly from the offices of the West Virginia Department of Education.[9]

Another ACA strategy was to provide political cover for state leaders by arranging for the coal owners' associations to pay their own corporate attorneys to prosecute striking miners *on behalf of the state*, then later bill taxpayers $125,000 for their prosecutorial services.[10]

In July 1922, the *New York Times* featured Conley's propaganda guild aggressively defending what it admits was "the state mine guard system."

To promote Conley's Golden Horseshoe Society at its inception, West Virginia School Superintendent William C. Cook stated that for students to become West Virginia's best citizens, they "should have knowledge of the past and present status of the state in order to estimate its future possibilities." Unfortunately when granting extraction industry leaders the unfettered ability to distort or otherwise bury the historic record of their excesses, Cook neglected to predict the dire effect Conley's "Society" would have on the future of the state's citizenry.[11]

Thanks to the combined efforts of state leaders and their coal industry backers to cover up the history of oppression throughout West Virginia, it may never be determined just how widely the Esau system was used to terrorize the families of struggling laborers.[12]

Human rights organizations have defined rape as a weapon of war, used effectively to isolate families and control entire communities. It has often been diagnosed as systemic where paternalistic societies have fallen under military rule. Leading up to West

MINE GUARD UPHELD BY WEST VIRGINIA

State, Through Press Agent,

Denies Stories of Lawlessness and Starvation.

West Virginia now has a press agent. An organization which calls itself the American Constitutional Association, with headquarters at Charleston, W. Va., in a statement issued here yesterday announced that it was out to "correct the false impression which prevails concerning our commonwealth."

Need for the propaganda work is emphasized by the association because "throughout the United States people are thinking that we are only partly civilized, that our government has fallen down, and that life is held very cheap." The association charges that persons are being paid for "consistently criticising the State of West Virginia," to scare away industries that threaten to leave other States to be near the fuel supply.

"Obviously it pays well," it was added, "to keep the directors of large industrial concerns believing that West Virginia has continuous labor trouble, that the Government of the State has broken down, and that we have a hotbed of lawlessness."

In defense of the mine guard system, the association said:

"The one thing that has been emphasized more than any other by outsiders is the so-called deputy sheriff or mine guard system. One is led to believe that West Virginia originated and has a monopoly on an unique plan, and that all other States are so highly civilized that they would not tolerate anything like it. The facts are that the same system is used in New York, Pennsylvania, Colorado, and in every other industrial State. Why is this system such a horrible thing for West Virginia and of so much value to the industries of the other States?"

Deploring the many investigations of conditions and reports of starving miners, the statement concluded:

"We venture the opinion that among our 1,400,000 citizens there are less people needing assistance than can be found in a score of blocks in New York City."

The New York Times
Published: July 31, 1922

The American Constitutional Association

Soon after the uprising at Blair Mountain, powerful coal owners and politicians banded together not just to keep coal laborers from collective bargaining, but to erase the sordid history of the state's complicity of upholding the coal industry policy of terrorizing the public.

While it is true that corporations in other states paid gun thugs to break strikes, other governors had never ordered printing presses destroyed or editors jailed.

Virginia's mine wars, virtually all of West Virginia's southern coal camps were paternalistic, in many ways similar to pre–Civil War southern cotton plantations. Coal owners were successful in their oppression only through the widespread use of their brutal private military, operating for years under the full consent of the state.[13]

During the battle at Blair, federal military officers were escorted to Logan County by local UMW leaders to assess the situation and to determine whether or not federal troops should be dispatched to the battlefield. A member of that group recalled, "The women seemed to say more than the men. They did not want the men to go back unless the United States troops were there to see that they were protected." Testifying under oath regarding the attitude of marchers in the field, that same team member (David Fowler) quoted a woman from Ramage (near Blair) who, when confronted with Governor Morgan's order for the redneck army to disband, had exclaimed to him, "My God, Mr. Fowler, it would be all right if it were the union's affair, and we would say nothing; but it is not the union's affair and the people of West Virginia are here to protect their honor."[14]

That very same year at one of the hundreds of "teaching institutes" established by Conley's ACA throughout West Virginia, Mineral County teachers denounced the "Bolshevistic tendencies" of their fellow West Virginians who were coal laborers, recommending the "comprehensive teaching of Americanism, good citizenship, and morality to alleviate the problem."[15]

Through the ACA Conley successfully provided political cover for the coal owners' association across the Kanawha field, which, in an industry-wide sweep starting in 1922, began evicting from company housing as many as 10,000 union miners, or 50,000 people including the miners' families. These refugees were replaced with strikebreakers.[16]

Over the short term Phil Conley's propaganda campaign effectively delayed the result intended by those who had marched to battle. The reign of terror by coal owners, as sanctioned by the State of West Virginia, didn't end until 1933 when it literally took an act of Congress to restore civil liberties back to miners and their families. Only ninety days after Roosevelt's National Industrial Recovery Act was passed, West Virginia's southern coalfields were essentially unionized.[17]

West Virginia was very likely the first state in U.S. history to have been investigated by Congress for labor violations by the state's own government. Although the U.S. Senate committee revealed that the state's governor and its lower courts had been violating the constitutional rights of citizens as early as 1912 and recommended abolishing the mine guard system, the committee failed to reestablish justice due to its lack of jurisdiction. Source: U.S. Senate, Committee on Education and Labor, Investigation of Paint Creek Coal Fields of West Virginia, *report pursuant to S. Res. 37, Senate report 321, 63d Cong. 2d sess., March 9, 1914.*

In 2010, respected West Virginia historian and author David Alan Corbin spoke to a gathering hosted by the West Virginia Humanities Council. Not far from the Capital Complex in Charleston, Corbin spoke mainly of Matewan's heroic Police Chief Sid Hatfield and the galvanizing effect that his assassination had on the entire labor movement. Corbin also recalled the startling results of an informal survey that he'd taken decades earlier at a large central high school in the southern part of the state.

Calling for a show of hands, Corbin had begun his survey by asking, "How many here know about America's largest armed rebellion since the Civil War?" Although the school auditorium had been packed with students and teachers from the entire school for a lecture, there was no response. Trying a second time,

Corbin dropped a clue, adding that thousands of armed miners had marched to battle in the same county that the auditorium they were in was located. Recalling that his clue had grabbed everyone's attention, Corbin confessed that he'd been shocked to find that no one in the room seemed even aware of the Battle of Blair Mountain, much less of its unique historic importance.[18]

In Charleston at the West Virginia Humanities Council lecture, Corbin ended his recollection of the survey by publicly criticizing state education officials for having purposely repressed what may well be the richest labor history of any state in the nation.

"In 12 years in public schools in West Virginia, I, like others of my generation, never heard a thing about the great West Virginia Mine Wars," Corbin explained. "In high school, our textbook, *West Virginia: Yesterday and Today*, discussed the importance of the coal industry to our state, but made no mention of coal miners. Nothing about the United Mine Workers."[19]

The state's active attempt to eliminate its own darkest actions from recorded history became most obvious during the administration of West Virginia governor Homer Adams Holt. While in office, he kept Roosevelt's badly needed New Deal Works Progress Administration money from flowing into the state until Roosevelt administrators agreed to purge the historic West Virginia Guide of an entire chapter on labor history. To this day Holt's strident efforts to erase the state's support of systemic corporate terrorism are excluded from his online bio as presented by the West Virginia Division of Culture and History. Nor can his revisionist efforts be found by searching the state's official online encyclopedia.[20]

Homer Holt not only viewed the struggles of labor and all reports of the cruelty of corporate avarice as "subversive," he did everything within his power to keep it out of the texts of his day. Years earlier Governor Hatfield, a Republican, had destroyed the printing presses of labor newspapers; then later Governor Holt, a

Democrat, established the state Publicity Commission to counter the "negative publicity" from Hatfield's era and to promote his own interpretation of historic events for West Virginia.[21]

No matter how well intentioned the authors of biased revisionism may have been, there can be dire results if generations of citizens are kept from understanding the whole truth.

At a recent press conference regarding the UMWA report on the explosion that killed twenty-nine mine workers at Montcoal, West Virginia's Upper Big Branch Mine, Union President Cecil Roberts shattered the popular misconception that all deep mines were "accidents waiting to happen," a notion that had been wrongly promoted by the coal industry for years. Introducing the union's own incident report, which, in its very title tags the Upper Big Branch fatalities as "Industrial Homicide," Roberts made it clear that the term "accident" should never be misapplied to what caused that explosion. The UMWA Executive Summary reports the following: "The dangerous conditions that contributed to the explosion existed at the mine on a daily basis. These conditions, which represented gross violations of mandatory health and safety standards, were *not accidental.*" (italics added).[22]

In contrast, the U.S. Department of Labor's Mine Safety and Health Administration (MSHA) used the term "accident" eighteen times within its ten-page Executive Summary alone, making it far more difficult to blame government officials for not shutting that mine down over the long-term pattern of obvious safety violations.[23]

The first report to be made public after the explosion was by a team of independent experts. Led by former MSHA head J. Davitt McAteer, it charged that the blast was, in no small part, *due to the inability of the state of West Virginia to protect the lives of miners.* Appropriately calling it "a political failure—a failure by the state's government to nurture and support strict safety standards for coal miners," the scathing 120-page study recommended (in part) that, "If miners' lives are to be safeguarded, the cozy relationship between high-ranking government officials and the coal industry must change, as must the relationship between the enforcement agency and the industry it regulates." While the UMWA's Executive Summary "wholeheartedly agrees" with that assessment, both MSHA and the West Virginia Office of Miners' Health Safety and Training completely failed to address the issue.[24]

There is one point upon which all of the investigators of Upper Big Branch universally agree: *If existing regulations had only been enforced, the deadly explosion at Upper Big Branch could have been avoided.*

In his *Charleston Gazette* article "Reforms Written in Miners' Blood," Paul J. Nyden wrote, "When people talk about the history of mine safety, there is 'before Farmington,' and there is 'after Farmington.'"

"'Up until then, there was no rock dusting, no controlling the mine dust, which is basically gunpowder,' said Gov. Joe Manchin, whose uncle John died in explosions that rocked Farmington No. 9 mine before dawn on Nov. 20, 1968."[25] Even though Manchin lived in Farmington and was certainly old enough at the time of the incident to recall it, his details regarding rock dusting were completely inaccurate. Just after the blast, the executive vice president for operations for Consolidated Coal Corp. admitted to reporters that "the workings [at Farmington No. 9] were heavily rock-dusted, which may account for the lack of fire and violence at the 'front' of the mine from which the 21 men escaped safely."[26]

Many years had passed since the Farmington disaster, yet just after the Upper Big Branch disaster Manchin quite explicitly recalled other details of the Farmington blast, almost as if he had been in the mine with his uncle, stating, "These were horrific explosions. The air was so bad. The fires were so hot." Manchin recalled. "There was no way mine rescuers, the bravest people I have ever been around, could go past certain points."[27]

It is important to note that the "certain points" to which Manchin referred were areas where the company had apparently chosen *not* to implement rock dusting. Consol could make that choice at Farmington because it was before regulations required rock dusting. Massey's Upper Big Branch Mine near Montcoal hadn't rock dusted despite *existing* regulations that the state should have enforced *while Joe Manchin was governor.*

In all fairness, Manchin could have been mistaken about the rock dusting at Farmington because just after the incident West Virginia governor Hulett C. Smith had told reporters, "I would like to explain that this is an accident," pointedly adding, "I have confidence that the mining industry is seeing the most improved safety measures are being taken. We have experienced tragedy here many times before. Mining is a hazardous profession."[28]

Despite Governor Smith's reassurances that West Virginia's coal operators had been doing all they possibly could to prevent "accidents" from happening, lawmakers nonetheless passed the long overdue Coal Mine Health and Safety Act of 1969. Had Manchin's regulators simply enforced that law at Upper Big Branch, the deadliest explosion in any West Virginia coal operation since Farmington would have been avoided. Yet despite the McAteer panel's recommendation to do away with the "cozy relationship" between coal owners and political leaders, *at this writing virtually nothing has changed to keep another such "accident" from happening again.*[29]

Even historians and educators seeking to honestly portray the past frequently fall into the habit of using terms and contexts that distort the reality of events as they occurred. Today they speak and write of the Matewan Massacre, which wasn't a massacre at all but a shootout that took place when Matewan Police Chief Sid Hatfield attempted to force a group of coal owners' mercenaries to surrender their guns inside his jurisdiction. Witness accounts agree that both sides had weapons and both sides suffered casualties. Yet the West Virginia Division of Culture and History's Archives and History section repeatedly refers to the incident as the "Matewan Massacre," and on its website is featured an unidentified newspaper piece that improperly portrays the event as an ambush instead of a showdown. Titled "Matewan Massacre," the article was copied directly from a news clipping in the archived Logan Coal Association Collection and prominently placed online without proper identification of the source.[30] The lack of any correction or proper attribution speaks volumes about the state-paid historians who chose to feature it.

The West Virginia Department of Education has long encouraged students to use West Virginia's online State Archives and internet links, and to visit the state's multimillion-dollar "museum" at the Capitol Complex Cultural Center to study for "noted" historian Phil Conley's Golden Horseshoe accolade. Few, if any, are ever made aware by their teachers that the state's official website has been seeded with the deceptions of a hardcore industrial propagandist.

Phil Conley passed away years ago, but thanks to the West Virginia Division of Culture and History, his legacy still claims victims, buries evidence, and exonerates murderers.

West Virginia's natural resources are more bountiful than most any other state in the entire country. By burying the truth throughout the last century, news editors, politicians, and their well-heeled financiers have successfully kept the state's natural born citizens among the poorest and least educated in the nation.

Notes

1. Joe Geiger, "Golden Horseshoe," *West Virginia Archives and History News* vol. 5, no. 1 (March 2004): 1.

2. West Virginia Department of Education Golden Horseshoe website, at http://wvde.state.wv.us/goldenhorseshoe/about.html (Accessed June 1, 2017).

3. Erica Green, "Blair Mountain Battle Continues," NPR news broadcast, June 16, 2010.

4. National Historic Landmark Theme Study on American Labor History pursuant to Public Law 102-101 (1991).

5. Ibid.

6. Cecil Roberts testimony before the U.S. House Committee on Mining and Natural Resources, February 21, 1991. Quoted in James Green, *Taking History to Heart* (Amherst: University of Massachusetts Press, 2000), 147–65, which includes a fuller examination of sites of conflict in the South.

7. John C. Hennen, *The Americanization of West Virginia: Creating a Modern Industrial State, 1916–1925* (Lexington: University Press of Kentucky, 1966), 126.

8. William C. Blizzard, *When Miners March*, ed. Wess Harris (Oakland, CA: PM Press, 2010), 357.

9. Hennen, *The Americanization of West Virginia*, 126.

10. Richard D. Lunt, *Law and Order vs. the Miners: West Virginia, 1907–1933* (Hamden, CT: Archon Books, 1979), 158–59.

11. Geiger, "Golden Horseshoe"; West Virginia Board of Education website, at http://wvde.state.wv.us/ (Accessed June 1, 2017).

12. See Michael and Carrie Kline, "Esau in the Coalfields" in this volume, 5–25. Originally in *Appalachian Heritage* vol. 59, no. 5 (Summer 2011).

13. *Paternalism*, a Pocahontas Coal Operators' Association pamphlet: UMWA District 17 files UMWA archives, UMWA Headquarters, Washington, DC; Jocelyn Kelly, "Rape in War: Motives of Militia in DRC," U.S Institute of Peace Special Report 243, (June 2010); Laura Smith-Spark, "How did rape become a weapon of war?" BBC News Special (December 8, 2004).

14. Testimony: David Fowler, Red Jacket v John L. Lewis, 2: 2863.

15. Hennen, *The Americanization of West Virginia*, 126.

16. Lunt, *Law and Order vs. the Miners*, 166.

17. Ibid., 181.

18. Tom Rhule's personal notes and transcripts of an audio recording of Corbin's lecture.

19. Paul J. Nyden, "Historian Brings Mine Wars Back to Life," *Charleston Gazette*, May 23, 2010.

20. Jerry B. Thomas, "'The Nearly Perfect State': Governor Homer Adams Holt, the WPA Writers' Project and the Making of West Virginia: A Guide to the Mountain State," *West Virginia History* vol. 52 (1993): 91–108.

21. Ibid.

22. United Mine Workers of America, Executive Summary, *Industrial Homicide: Report on the Upper Big Branch Mine Disaster*, 13

23. Executive Summary, *U.S. Department of Labor's Mine Safety and Health Administration (MSHA) on Upper Big Branch Mine Disaster*.

24. West Virginia Governor's Independent Investigation Panel Report on Upper Big Branch, May 19, 2011.

25. Paul J. Nyden, "Reforms Written in Miners' Blood," *Charleston Gazette*, November 23, 2008.

26. "78 Miners Entombed in Farmington No. 9 after Blasts Rip Workings," *Times West Virginian*, November 21, 1968, at http://www.wvculture.org/history/disasters/farmington02.html (Accessed June 1, 2017).

27. Nyden, "Reforms Written in Miners' Blood."

28. "78 Miners Entombed in Farmington No. 9 after Blasts Rip Workings."

29. Ken Ward Jr., "Drug Testing Bill 'a Distraction,' McAteer Says," *Charleston Gazette*, February 7, 2012.

30. "Matewan Massacre," unidentified article, Logan Coal Operators Association Collection, http://www.wvculture.org/history/labor/matewan04.html.

Appalachian Scholar

Walter Lane

I hear our articulate, self-appointed authority's loud voice.
He has a PhD from the University of
Somewhere Else, a prestigious university.
He has written the definitive history of the
Mt. Dream Area, he says,
Which he sells to his unwilling students at a war price.
The state newspaper has anointed him
a true scholar of Appalachia.
Appalachian regional magazines have excerpted his work.
And the local people mumble "fraud"—
Mutes in the world of scholars,
I tell friends of my flea market–purchased
Anthropology book, which tells of
Bongo-bongoism—a vice of a scholar who
works among natives not articulate
enough to provide a scholarly rebuttal.
So I scratch on a discarded legal pad
protests about these new imperialists
out to strip mine our heritage,
                                    our traditions
for their own profit.

Walter Lane is a former miner, social commentator, and poet who currently lives within mailing distance of Raccoon, Kentucky.

Battle of Blair Mountain Pamphlet
Logan District Mines Information Bureau

The following 15 pages reveal an unadulterated perspective from the coal operator's union.

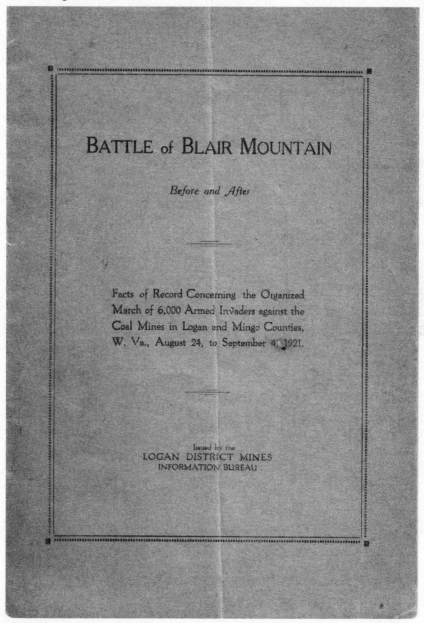

BATTLE of BLAIR MOUNTAIN

Before and After

Facts of Record Concerning the Organized
March of 6,000 Armed Invaders against the
Coal Mines in Logan and Mingo Counties,
W. Va., August 24, to September 4, 1921.

Issued by the
LOGAN DISTRICT MINES
INFORMATION BUREAU

Statement of
GOVERNOR E. F. MORGAN,
of West Virginia

———

"I have not participated and am not interested in the program of the United Mine Workers of America in extending their organization into the non-union coal fields of West Virginia.

"I have not participated and am not interested in the efforts of the coal operators in the non--union fields in opposing unionization.

"I AM INTERESTED, however, both as an official and a citizen in the maintenance of law and the preservation of order, and all the force at my command will be used to require those engaged in labor strife, whether operator or miner, union or non-union, to obey the laws of the State."

BATTLE *of* BLAIR MOUNTAIN

THROUGHOUT the seventeen years during which commercial coal has been mined in the Logan district of West Virginia, strikes, shut-downs or other labor troubles have been practically unknown in this flourishing field.

Similarly, industrial peace reigned in Mingo county, adjoining Logan on the southwest, until the spring of 1920 when refusal of the coal producers to negotiate contracts with the United Mine Workers of America was followed by repeated acts of lawlessness. Martial law was then proclaimed throughout the district, and thereafter has remained in force.

As soon as martial law was proclaimed, the United Mine Workers established tent colonies for its members in the district. The last census as of July 18, 1821, records a tent colony population of 1304 men, women and children living in idleness while enjoying weekly payments from the treasury of the United Mine Workers.

Adjoining Logan county on the northeast is Boone county, where the mine workers are organized. Kanawha county, in which mobilization for the armed invasion of Aug. 24---Sept. 4 took place, adjoins Boone county, and also is organized.

It will thus be seen that Logan county was the "Belgium" of the attempted invasion. On the crest of a mountain range dividing Logan and Boone, defenders took their positions to check the oncoming rush of the invaders. An Associated Press dispatch dated Washington, Sept. 17, refers to the invasion as follows:

> "It was in protest against the enforcement of martial lay and to compel unionization of the Mingo county mines that the miners' army started its march, stopping only when Federal troops intervened."

The Logan mine owners and their employes started operations on Thanksgiving Day, 1904, working under a non-union agreement. This agreement—never disputed by employes or producers—has continued in uninterrupted force. Industrial harmony has blessed the region. Now, as in past years, union miners are given employment without prejudice, the only stipulation being that they refrain from exploiting their union affiliation while working in the Logan field. Approximately 50 per cent of Logan workers on today's payrolls are men who formerly held active membership in the United Mine Workers of America.

The Logan district mines produce about 35 per cent of West Virginia's total output of coal, from non-union mines. Approximately one-tenth of all the bituminous coal mined in the world comes from West Virginia fields. Domination of the present non-union fields by the United Mine Workers of America would place that organization in industrial command of the bituminous situation.

Governor Morgan describes the recent attempted invasion as "an organized outbreak against the law and constituted authorities in the southern section of this State (West Virginia)". Newspapers throughout the country called it the "March Against Logan and Mingo," and referred to the several days' bitter fighting as the "Battle of Blair Mountain."

A score or more of men were killed. Many were wounded. The invaders took possession of trains carrying United States mails; forced unwilling men and boys to join their ranks; looted stores; and ignored President Harding's proclamation calling upon them to disperse and disarm. United States army troops were sent to the scene in response to Governor Morgan's appeal for Federal aid. The cost of transporting and maintaining these troops is placed at more than $1,000,000. Loss in wages to the Kanawha district miners, and loss to the Kanawha district producers because of the virtual closing down of all work, totaled an estimated loss of more than $500,000 up to September 4.

Both the Logan and Kanawha districts are served by the Chesapeake & Ohio Railroad. The official loading reports of the C. & O. recorded during the period of the attempted invasion, supplies proof of how the earnings of the miners in the Logan and Kanawha districts were effected. Under normal conditions, production in the respective fields is substantially the same—about 750 cars per day each.

The miners are paid on the amount of tonnage produced. The C. & O. reports are based on 50-ton car shipments. Following are the daily shipments from Aug. 19 to Sept. 9, inclusive—supplying proof of the extent to which men from the organized field in Kanawha district participated in the invasion:

Date	Logan Dist. Cars	Kanawha Dist. Cars
Aug. 19	661	410
" 22	626	211
" 23	552	299
" 24	610	214
" 25	541	184
" 26	791	152
" 27	423	38
" 29	697	25
" 30	462	133
" 31	453	180
Sept. 1	451	122
" 2	511	125
" 3	458	67
" 5	725	61
" 7	637	267
" 8	712	405
" 9	696	492
Total....	10,006 cars	3,385 cars
	500,300 tons	169,250 tons

The above table shows that during the height of the trouble the Logan miners were paid for producing 331,050 more tons of coal than the Kanawha miners, enabling the distribution of more than three times the amount of wages in the Logan district as compared with the Kanawha field.

The 6,000 or more men who took part in the armed invasion mobilized in Kanawha and Boone counties, and recruits came from Fayette and Raleigh counties which comprise the New River District. The mine owners in these fields operate under contract with the United Mine Workers of America. District 17, U. M. W. of A., with headquarters in Charleston, capital of West Virginia, has jurisdiction over the State. C. F. Keeney is president, and Fred Mooney, secretary, of District 17.

At the time of the invasion there was no controversy of any nature whatsoever between the Kanawha, Boone, Raleigh and Fayette county producers and their employes. No strike existed—none was impending.

The Kanawha Coal Operators Association, having as members the mine owners of these counties, acts in matters of mutual interest between employes and employers.

Early in August, Association members reported that their employes were not living up to the contracts entered into with the United Mine Workers of America. The miners had submitted no grievances. The subject of wage reductions had not been raised. In view of conditions which the union producers said were becoming alarming, the following letter was prepared and forwarded:

"Mr. C. F. Keeney, Pres.,
District 17, U. M. W. of A.,
Charleston, W. Va.

Dear Sir.—

I am writing you to protest against the serious situation existing in the Kanawha district, occasioned by members of your organization.

For the last two weeks men have been traveling over this district meeting with members of the committees at the various coal mines, agitating men to congregate, in certain parts of this district, which has been done. Complaints are coming into this office from practically all over the district that mines have been closed in violation of contract.

It is unnecessary for me to state to you the situation existing in this district, and the high cost of producing coal resulting. These unwarranted shut-downs only aggravate the tense situation and further increase the cost of production.

We have refrained, so far, from asking you to amend our contract looking toward a reduction in wages, and we must insist upon your organization doing everything in your power to insist upon your membership complying with the contract that exists between the operators and miners of this district.

I trust it will be your pleasure to immediately get in touch with the situation and correct the abuses complained of.

Very truly yours,

(Signed) D. C. KENNEDY,
Sec'y-Comm'r Kanawha Coal Operators Association."

Keeney made no reply to this letter, a copy of which was sent to John Lewis, international president of the United Mine Workers of America. Lewis replied as follows:

"Indianapolis, Ind.,
August 24, 1921.

Mr. D. C. Kennedy, Sec'y-Comm'r
Kanawha Coal Operators Association,
Kanawha Valley Bank Building,
Charleston, W. Va.

Dear Sir:—

I am in receipt of your letter of Aug. 22, transmitting copy of communication which you have addresssed to President Keeney of District 17 on the same date. I advise that the subject matter will be given every consideration by this office.

Yours very truly,
(Signed) JOHN L. LEWIS, President,
United Mine Workers of America."

Except for the above letter, no further communication was received from Lewis.

Briefly stated the reasons for the attempted invasion of Mingo county through Logan county, are as follows:

When in July, 1920, the Mingo mines decided to continue a non-union agreement with their men, the United Mine Workers called a strike. Lawlessness ensued. The Tug river, separating Mingo county from Kentucky, is about fifty feet from bank to bank. Rifle and pistol

PROSPEROUS MINERS BUILT   UP THIS BUSINESS CENTRE

SEVENTEEN years of uninterrupted thrift and contentment have established Logan, West Virginia, in a unique and enviable position among the coal centres of this country. Freedom from strikes, shutdowns and other labor disturbances that have afflicted neighboring districts, has enabled Logan wage-earners to enjoy high standards of living. Their demands for high-grade clothing, food and home comforts have attracted wide-awake merchants to Logan. Modern stores (as you see in the above photo) occupy the sites along Logan's crowded business streets.

HOME-MAKERS in this flourishing community attribute their prosperity to working conditions under the American or open-shop plan. The miners have subscribed to this plan year after year, although about 50 per cent of their total number formerly were active members of union organizations. More than a quarter of the total deposits in Logan banks represent miners' savings. Among other things, seventy-two miles of railroad extensions have been built out of Logan since the first coal was shipped from there in 1904.

firing was directed from the Kentucky side of the Tug, thus involving Kentucky authority. By joint request of the Governors of Kentucky and West Virginia, martial law was declared in Mingo county. Since the issuance of the proclamation, crime in Mingo county has decreased more than 90 per cent.

"It was the enforcement of martial law in Mingo county," Governor Morgan says, "that was cited as a reason for the mobilization of the armed miners of Kanawha and Boone counties, who were later joined by armed bands from some of the mines in Raleigh and Fayette Counties.

"IT WAS ANNOUNCED THAT THE OBJECTIVE OF THE MARCH WAS TO RESIST MARTIAL LAW IN MINGO COUNTY.

"The insurrectionists exhibited their antipathy toward lay enforcement officers on August 12, near Sharples, Boone county, when an armed body of sixty men held-up, disarmed and robbed two State policemen, and ordered them to leave Boone county. On the night of August 19, at Edwight, an attempt was made to assassinate another State policeman.

He was shot in the back by an armed body of men which left Edwight the following morning for Lens creek. These armed bodies continued to assemble on Lens Creek (about ten miles from Charleston), patrolling the roads, halting and using railroad trains, pillaging stores of arms, ammunition and supplies, and invading private homes in search of guns."

During the week beginning August 14, agitators visited the mining camps in the Kanawha and adjacent districts and in public speeches told the United Mine Workers to prepare for the invasion of Logan and Mingo. Between 200 and 300 men had assembled at Marmet, on Lens creek on August 20. From this number, delegates were sent back to each mine in the Kanawha field bearing tidings that the armed march was about to start. "Orders" were given to United Mine Workers to arm and report at Marmet. Guards were posted along the roads leading to Marmet.

On the night of Wednesday, August 24, between 3000 and 4000 armed men were assembled. The advance started. Governor Morgan describes the situation at this stage as follows:

> "The officers of Kanawha county advised me they were unable to cope with the situation or disperse the insurgents, and on the following day I requested Federal troops. I felt that Federal troops were necessary because the National Guard (disbanded following the world war) had not yet been reorganized under a law that had been effective for less than thirty days, and the State police were engaged in the enforcement of martial law in Mingo county and distributed at their stations in various parts of the State. (The total roster of State Police at this time was about 100 men).

"MY OPTION WAS TO ASK FOR FEDERAL TROOPS OR ASK FOR CITIZEN VOLUNTEERS TO REPEL THE INVASION. TO SAVE BLOODSHED, I CHOSE TO ASK THE FEDERAL GOVERNMENT FOR TROOPS."

Instead of sending troops, Secretary of War Weeks ordered Brigadier-General H. H. Bandholtz to the scene. On his arrival, Gen Bandholtz conferred with Keeney and Mooney and other officers of the United Mine Workers, demanding that they proceed forthwith to Madison where the armed march had halted after advancing about forty-five miles from Charleston. The demand was obeyed. The march was stopped. All except about 1,200 of the 6,000 armed men who composed the "army" at this time, scattered in the mountains. They took with them machine guns, high-power rifles, thousands of rounds of ammunition, and provisions.

The following night, August 27, Captain J. R. Brockus, of the State Police and a squad of men crossed the Logan line from Mingo into Boone county, near Sharples, to serve warrants on forty men wanted by Sheriff Don Chafin, of Logan county. Proceeding down Beech creek, Brockus encountered armed men patrolling the roads. Two patrols surrendered. A third answered Brockus' commands with a volley of bullets. The fire was returned. Three men were killed during the encounter.

News of the fight was carried by the miners' couriers to the men who had turned back from the invasion, supposedly for their homes.

Within twenty-four hours, more than 6,000 armed men had assembled with headquarters at Jeffrey. Under army-like formation, they advanced toward the rugged mountains separating Blair from Logan.

Meantime, word of the renewed invasion had sped through the southwest territory of the state. Volunteers from many sections started for Logan on the double-quick to aid in resisting the advance. An example of the personnel of this volunteer force is contained in the following resolution later passed by McDowell county authorities:

> "The citizens of this county, miners, American Legion members, doctors, lawyers, merchants, bankers, laborers, clerks and others, 1229 in number, upon the call of the Governor, nobly responded as volunteers in defense of the laws of the country."

In the van of volunteers from the Pocahontas field were three score American Legion members. Charleston business and professional men added their quotas.

The volunteer army of defense took up positions along a 15-mile line on the mountain crests about two miles west of Blair. Attack followed attack by the invad-

ers.   "No Man's Land" was swept by machine gun bullets
and the fire of sharpshooters.   The fighting continued
almost unceasingly for four days.   On September 2, Federal troops arrived in the State, some of them taking up
positions in Logan, others proceeding to Madison, Sharples, Jeffrey, Clothier and Blair.   As the troops advanced, detachments of the miners surrendered and dis-
persed.   But even while the troops occupied the area,
some of the heaviest fighting of the invasion was taking
place at the front.   The troops were forced to penetrate
to advanced positions before the dispersal became general.   A majority of the miners did not bring their arms
with them when they surrendered.

At no time did the defenders seek to advance.   Efforts
were centered on keeping the insurrectionists from invading Logan.

Much has been said about the so-called "mine guards"
in the Logan field.   Logan county comprises 400 square
miles with a population of 60,000.   Law enforcement
over this far-flung area is maintained by eight consta-
bles, and as many State Police as occasion requires.   Of
the later, half a dozen were on duty at the time of the
attempted invasion.   When fighting started, however,
less than a hundred others were rushed to the scene.
Prior to August 24, twenty-four deputy sheriffs were on
duty in Logan.   Through an arrangement with the County Court of Logan, the mining companies were paying the
salaries of 19 deputies although these deputies serving
under the Sheriff of Logan county, collected taxes and per-
formed similar duties.   They neither came into contact
with, nor had authority over the miners in the day's work.

They received a small extra compensation for the extra work of guarding the mines' semi-monthly payroll. This payroll called for the disbursal of about $500,000 in cash every two weeks. Because of insurance requirements, the deputies guarded this cash in the absence of other law-enforcement officers.

Prior to the acceptance of a deputy, the Circuit Judge passes on the candidate's character and demands a bond for the privilege of carrying arms. The financial burden of deputy-sheriff employment will be spared mine owners as soon as the State carries out its law enforcement pro-gramme now nearing completion. Until then—as during past years—the protection of life and property must be undertaken by the mine owners in the only way provided by law.

At the time of the attempted invasion, Keeney and Mooney were fugitives from justice, indictments having been returned against them in Williamson, Mingo county, on charges of murder in connection with a shooting affray in Mingo county last May.

On Sept. 17, Keeney, Mooney and W. H. Blizzard, who is alleged to have led the attempted invasion, were among 500 men indicted at Logan on charges of murder, insur-rection or carrying weapons. Of this number, about 400 are charged specifically with murder.

The murder indictments returned were based on the Red Man Act. Section 10 of the Act reads:

"If two or more persons under the name of 'Red Men', 'regulators', Vigilance Committee', or any other name or without a name, combine or conspire together for the pur-pose of destroying, injuring, or taking and carrying away any property, real of personal, not their own, every such person whether he has done any act in pursuance of such combination or conspiracy or not, shall be guilty of a misdemeanor and fined not less than fifty, nor more than five hundred dollars. and may, at the discretion of the court, be confined in jail not less than one or more than twelve months."

Section 13 reads:

"If the death of any person shall result from the commission of any offense mentioned in the tenth section of this chapter, every person engaged in the commission of such offense shall be guilty of murder of the first degree, and punished as in other cases of murder of the first degree."

Keeney and Mooney surrendered in Charleston on Sept. 18 and were taken to the Williamson jail. John L. Lewis immediately communicated with Governor Morgan as follows:

"In view of the fact that President C. F. Keeney and Secretary-Treasurer Fred Mooney, of District 17, United Mine Workers of America, have surrendered to the authorities of West Virginia in answer to grand jury indictments previously rendered against them, I sincerely hope that your office will take every necessary step to insure the safety of their persons and lives. This request is necessitated by the fact that formerly members of the United Mine Workers of West Virginia who became prisoners of the commonwealth were subjected to personal indignities resulting in certain instances in loss of life. The mine workers of the country sincerely hope that the authority of your office will be ample to protect Messrs. Keeney and Mooney from circumstances of this character. I also express the hope that similar treatment will be accorded all members of the United Mine Workers of America now imprisoned or under indictment in West Virginia."

Replying to the above communication, Governor Morgan said:

"Your appeal to the constituted authorities of this State follows within a few hours of your public statement that the State government of West Virginia had broken down. Your belated recognition that our government is functioning is complete refutation of your previous statement. Keeney and Mooney, of course, will have the protection of the authorities. However,
IF YOU HAD SHOWN THE SAME SOLICITATION FOR THE POOR TOILING MEMBERS OF YOUR ORGANIZATION WHO WERE INCITED AND COERCED INTO INSURRECTION that you now display for its officers, Keeney and Mooney, many lives would have been saved, hundreds of members of your organization would not be standing under indictments, and the good name of West Virginia would not have been maligned from one end of this country to the other."

Food for thought . . .

C. Belmont Keeney's entry about Bill Blizzard in *The West Virginia Encyclopedia* states that "District 17 President [Frank] Keeney and Secretary-Treasurer Mooney managed [Blair Mountain Battle] events behind the scenes." On May 22, 2015, West Virginia Public Radio's Roxy Todd of *Inside Appalachia* asserted that President Keeney had "led the miners in the Battle of Blair Mountain." However, in his autobiography *Struggle in the Coal Fields,* UMWA Secretary-Treasurer Fred Mooney specifically recounted, "We kept in touch with developments through the press reports and by messenger." During the battle both Keeney and Mooney were in Ohio from 12:15 a.m. September 1 until September 16.

Since it is well established that from the outset of the conflict marchers cut area telephone and telegraph lines, and because there were no cell phones in 1921, it would have been physically impossible for Keeney to have actually led the Battle of Blair Mountain from Ohio. Furthermore, one of the main reasons state prosecutors dropped all charges against both Keeney and Mooney was because they were out of state and didn't return until after the battle.

So how could *The West Virginia Encyclopedia* and West Virginia Public Radio have gotten it so wrong? And why would they choose to downplay Bill Blizzard's leadership role?

Victory on Blair Mountain!

Wess Harris

Originally published in a slightly different form in Appalachian Heritage (vol. 59, no. 5, Summer 2011).

WHO REALLY WON THE BATTLE OF BLAIR MOUNTAIN? IN RETRO-spect it certainly wasn't the combined forces of the coal association and the state of West Virginia, as it has been wrongfully portrayed by the state's own historians and in the media. Considering the full context of the record as we know it today, all of the main goals for which the miners marched were accomplished. Though it took several years after the battle for the mine workers and their families to see the changes, few historians have ever recognized that this particular violent struggle in rural Appalachia was for far higher stakes than their "official" historical accounts ever originally claimed.

The first Battle of Blair Mountain, fought in 1921, was the largest armed insurrection since the Civil War. Logan County, West Virginia, saw a battle between ten thousand Union miners and their supporters determined to take the U.S. Constitution to southern West Virginia and perhaps half that many well-armed mercenaries fighting for the corporate interests seeking to keep unionization from the coalfields. The original battle was sparked by the murder of Matewan's pro-Union Chief of Police Sid Hatfield by Baldwin-Felts gun thugs in the employ of local coal operators. The real cause of the conflict ran much deeper.

Market pressures pitted labor costs in the heavily unionized northern coalfields against the nonunion southern fields. Perhaps most importantly, life in nonunion camps had become intolerable. This went far beyond merely wanting the Union. No longer would miners endure being told they could not visit with neighbors. No longer would miners suffer evictions, beatings, and even death for daring to speak their minds. No longer could miners tolerate coal companies forcing women into sexual servitude to keep their children from starving. It had become personal. There were scores to settle. The Union provided hope that the freedom and dignity won for the Europeans in the Great War and the promise of the U.S. Constitution could now become reality for the miners of southern West Virginia.

Today, the battle continues as coal companies want to mine the mountain using mountain removal technology that will destroy the mountain and, they hope, any memory of the earlier battle. The prevailing narrative that the Battle of Blair Mountain was a defeat for the miners is generally accepted by scholars, government agencies, coal companies, and even Union supporters looking back with pride on a noble but unsuccessful effort. Well-intentioned scholars, facing a wall of silence from miners maintaining a tradition of secrecy and a less than accurate spin from a variety of seemingly authoritative sources, have long repeated a tale of defeat that no longer withstands scrutiny. However pervasive and time-tested, this spin on events fails to meet the major requirement of any historical interpretation: external validity. The time has come to reevaluate standard interpretations of Blair Mountain and its significance.

Viewing the events on Blair Mountain as a "crushing defeat" for the miners (Meador, p. 63) is an understandable if fatally flawed interpretation resulting in no small part from a compartmentalization of our understanding of events: mine wars—Paint Creek, Cabin Creek, Blair Mountain—were fought and miners were defeated. Historian David Corbin observes that in the early 1930s, "Overnight, mine workers flocked to the union" (p. 161). This seemingly spontaneous organization appears as a unique event untied to the earlier "defeats." Providing a view of history that is internally consistent, externally valid, and of use to modern youth as they build a future mandates a major change of paradigm. From defeat to victory; from isolated mine wars to a fully connected thread, the Great West Virginia Mine War: 1890 to the present. Blair Mountain was not a distinct "mine war" that the Union lost, it was a battle the Union won.

Militarily, current knowledge leads to the inescapable conclusion that the Red Neck Army, Union miners wearing red bandanas as a uniform, was on the brink of victory with operators desperately calling for federal intervention. Archaeologist Brandon Nida offers the following take on the oft-imagined Union defeat:

> In our initial analysis, the archaeological evidence indicates that the miners were much more successful in their assault. Multiple sites have been discovered that show intense close quarter combat, with incoming bullet slugs and short range ammunition casings. All the evidence points to a different narrative than is usually told. Instead of the coal operator forces being able to hold off the miners but yet for some reason frantically calling for federal troops, the coal operators were instead frantically calling in the federal troops because their positions were being overrun by the miners.

Readers may wonder how it happened that 10,000 Union miners each possessed a red bandana to wear as identification in battle. Did not some prefer blue or white or yellow? While early miners were treated as contractors required to pay for their own tools and supplies, the ever-generous coal companies provided red—and only red—bandanas free of charge. All the better to mask the color of blood when, not if, injuries occurred!

Without question the intervention of federal troops brought about the end of fighting on Blair Mountain. In retrospect, the troops certainly did not come to further the Union cause. Yet not a shot was fired between the federal troops and the Red Neck Army. Bill Blizzard, leader of Union forces, actually approached the arriving troops. Miners, many veterans of the Great War and others, survivors of digging the coal that fed the American Navy, welcomed the arrival of "Our Boys." While one need not look far to find accounts describing the troops as suppressing the revolt or defeated miners surrendering, the reality at the time was likely quite different. Archaeologist Harvard Ayers, a longtime Blair Mountain researcher, is clear: "Absent the feds, I believe that the miners may have overrun the coal operators, and it would have been a bloody mess." When troops arrived, miners did not envision defeat. Far from surrendering, miners welcomed the troops as would any weary front line fighter being offered a chance to withdraw from the front and be replaced by fresh troops. Our Boys had arrived. Robert Shogan reminds us that as the miners marched from Blair Mountain, "many of them waved American flags" (p. 223). It is noteworthy that Blizzard, known but unnamed leader of the miners, was not arrested as would be any leader of a rebellion. He was free to go and allowed to keep his weapon. Hardly how a defeated rebel is treated!

Following the Battle and the disbursement of the Red Neck Army, hundreds of indictments were handed out to those who fought. Unable to defeat the Union on the field of battle, coal operators found it necessary to seek destruction of the Union using the courts. Not a single federal indictment was forthcoming but the Great State of West Virginia sought to hang Union leaders on charges ranging from arson to treason—against the state! A series of trials for Blizzard and others resulted in Union victory as they had been destined to win on the Mountain. While some minor convictions occurred, the trials resulted in acquittals for

Blizzard and other key figures. Not a single Union miner was hanged. Blizzard's execution could well have led to a similar fate for the leadership of other major American unions. A mere five years after the Russian Revolution, the leadership of the entire American labor movement was at risk. American capitalists were in no mood to coddle uppity workers. A change of venue resulted in the 1922 trials being held in the Eastern Panhandle town of Charles Town, West Virginia. Big Coal could not manage to rid themselves of Blizzard despite providing its own attorneys as prosecutors (Blizzard, pp. 322–23). When a verdict of acquittal came in, the citizens of Charles Town opened the American Legion Hall to make available fife and drum for a parade of celebration. Labor leaders around the country breathed a bit easier—and longer.

The prevailing "defeated" narrative views the decline of the Union in West Virginia throughout the 1920s as a result of the cost of the battle and the trials that followed. A depleted treasury could not support the cost of organizing. Seldom does West Virginia lead the nation, but throughout the '20s we were at the forefront of the Depression. Demand for coal and coal miners was low. Organizing against Big Coal was not likely to be successful no matter the resources available. Further, organizing in West Virginia throughout the '20s was hardly a priority for the Union. Rather than attempt to exploit the strong military showing on Blair Mountain and subsequent victories in the courts, International President John L. Lewis sought to consolidate his organizational control. David Corbin, writing in *The West Virginia Encyclopedia*, declares that Lewis "withdrew the autonomy of District 17, precipitating a collapse of the UMWA in southern West Virginia" (p. 480). To the extent that this collapse was a defeat, it was precipitated by the action of the international leadership of the Union, not by any actions of the miners on Blair Mountain or at the subsequent trials.

Only in 1932 did the Union reemerge as a major force in West Virginia. The nature of the resurgence sheds light on the meaning of the victory of Blair Mountain. Blizzard left the Union payroll shortly after the trials. John L. Lewis was not a fan of a grassroots leader who could prove tough to control and might become a rival. Yet throughout the 1920s Blizzard represented the Union as an unpaid lobbyist at the West Virginia state legislature. Indeed, from 1922 until 1955 he served the Union each session. In 1932, when FDR made unionization possible, Lewis recalled Blizzard to paid service for the Union. The military and legal victories of Blair Mountain began to show results.

Blair Mountain gave the people of the coalfields a hero in the person of Bill Blizzard. While some claimed that the absent District 17 officers Fred Mooney and Frank Keeney "managed events behind the scenes" (*West Virginia Encyclopedia*, p. 66) and others that Blizzard "did not command the army; he did not make its decisions or issue its orders. His acquittal in his later trial for treason demonstrated that" (Savage, p. 120). The miners knew better. They knew Mooney and Keeney lacked e-mail and wireless. Mooney makes it quite clear: "We kept in touch with developments through the press reports and by messenger until September 16" (p. 99). The miners kept a code of silence that shaded the events of Blair Mountain for decades. The victory of Blair Mountain is best understood as having three components: the Union was winning militarily, won in the courtroom, and most importantly, emerged with a leadership cadre that would go on to organize West Virginia in the early '30s and lead the miners of West Virginia until beyond midcentury.

John L. Lewis understood and hoped to harness and control the leadership treasure that came from Blair Mountain. We know in retrospect that Lewis was a classic autocrat in terms of leadership style. Blizzard, by contrast, emerged and remained very much of the grassroots. The two were oil and water, yet both spent their lives growing the same organization. In the early '30s, Lewis placed Blizzard back in District 17 to organize, and organize he did. But Lewis insured that he was on a short leash. Famed District 17 was Provisional District 17—provided John L. wanted it to be a district! (WCB, interviews, 2004–08). Bill was to serve under Van Bittner, whom Lewis imported from Pennsylvania to run the district and get credit for any organizing that occurred. If Blizzard did the organizing, Lewis controlled the credits. The last entry of Corbin's mine war anthology is of the August 1, 1933, *United Mine Workers Journal* article reporting on the June 23 convention in Charleston, which 2,500 miners attended. The article mentions Bittner no fewer than six times and Blizzard not once, yet it was Blizzard who made the convention happen (WCB). Lewis made certain that Blizzard would always be a supporting cast member. C.B. Keeney labels Blizzard a "protégé" or "close associate" of Bittner, yet nothing could be further from the truth (various editions, *West Virginia Encyclopedia*). Blizzard worked under Bittner in the organizational structure, but the hero of Blair Mountain was hardly a protégé of a chap from Pennsylvania who was absent from Blair Mountain, rode around in a Cadillac (preferably with a driver), kept a mistress on the top floor of a Charleston hotel, and expected the staff to call him "Boss." Blizzard drove himself around in a Chevy. Despite repeated attempts, this author could never get William C. Blizzard to agree that his father would so much as join Bittner for a social cup of coffee. Readers may judge which of the two were more likely to find a following among the coal diggers of West Virginia!

The years that follow Blair Mountain are far more meaningfully understood when we view the events of 1921–22 as victories rather than defeats. The cadre of leaders that emerged from the Battle—Blizzard and his lifelong friends Charley Payne, Ed Holstein, and others—would lead the Union in West Virginia for decades. Blizzard's grassroots popularity gave Lewis the membership numbers he needed to get those sweet contracts: pensions, health care, safety provisions, and the like. Blizzard got his status not because the Red Neck Army was defeated but because they were victors. It just took a few years to *look* like a win!

The great threat of the Red Neck Army and their strong showing on Blair Mountain, even as the International tried to stop the march, is the power of grassroots organizing. Power comes from either money or people and Blair Mountain was one battle that the people won. The operators, the government, and, sadly, even our Union for years tried to distort the meaning of events that occurred. Historians of all political leanings have all too often been complicit in repeating tales of defeat. Looking back, Blair Mountain was a victory by people no longer willing to be controlled, exploited, and violently abused from above. The Union miners of West Virginia were tired of losing; we were learning how to win.

Bibliography

Ayers, Harvard. Unpublished correspondence. Appalachian Community Services, Inc. Archives. Accessed April 27, 2011.

Blizzard, William C. Unpublished interviews with Wess Harris, 2004–2008.

Blizzard, William C. *When Miners March* ed. Wess Harris (Oakland, CA: PM Press, 2010).

Corbin, David Alan, ed. *The West Virginia Mine Wars: An Anthology* (Martinsburg, WV: Appalachian Editions, 1997).

Keeney, C.B. "Bill Blizzard," in *The West Virginia Encyclopedia* (Charleston: West Virginia Humanities Council, 2006).

Meador, Michael M. "The Red Neck War of 1921," in *The Goldenseal Book of the West Virginia Mine Wars* (Charleston, WV: Pictorial Histories, 1991).

Mooney, Fred *Struggle in the Coal Fields* (Morgantown: West Virginia University Library, 1967).

Nida, Brandon. Unpublished correspondence. Appalachian Community Services, Inc. Archives. Accessed August 17, 2011.

Savage, Lon. *Thunder in the Mountains: The West Virginia Mine War, 1920–21* (South Charleston, WV: Jalamap Publications, 1984).

Shogan, Robert. *Battle of Blair Mountain* (Boulder, CO: Westview Press, 2004).

Baseball and Treason

Bill Kovarik

Bill Kovarik is a professor of communication at Radford University. This article originally appeared in a slightly different form in Appalachian Voice.

Nothing can match it in the history of baseball. Check the team lineup: Bill Blizzard, right field. Charges: *Treason, murder*. Cecil Sullivan, first base. Charge: *Murder*. Okey Burgess, second base. Charge: *Murder*. W. Lacey, third base. Charge: *Treason*.

Bill Blizzard (with bat) pauses between court sessions for a publicity photo with his team. During the Battle of Blair Mountain and his trial Blizzard was portrayed by the coal owners and the local media as the "Generalissimo" who led a bloodthirsty army of bomb-throwing Bolsheviks.

The fans around the fields of Charles Town, West Virginia, knew that these were not minor leaguers. The stakes couldn't have been higher in the game that brought town residents and indicted union organizers together that spring of 1922.

The organizers were on trial for their roles in the Battle of Blair Mountain. A conviction on murder and treason charges would mean execution. The charges stemmed from an uprising against the coal industry following its assassination of Sid Hatfield, pro-union chief of police of Matewan.

Around thirty men had been killed in the uprising when the coal companies fought over 10,000 miners at the Battle of Blair Mountain in the spring of 1921. Now 200 miners were in Charles Town for trial. No one from the coal companies had faced similar indictments.

The coal companies demanded the death penalty for their opponents, and the State of West Virginia had been more than obliging, allowing coal company lawyers to prosecute the cases on its behalf. Even the indictments had been written in the law offices of the coal companies.

The companies assumed they could convince a Jefferson County jury that the union men were desperate traitors. At a time of national hysteria about the Bolshevik threat, a treason and murder trial against admitted insurrectionists must have seemed like an easy dinger—and maybe even a grand slam. They would legally execute dozens, jail thousands, and crush organized labor once and for all.

But the companies had made a serious mistake. Between court sessions, they were entertaining themselves at a swank out-of-town hotel. The accused union members, meanwhile, were playing baseball with the citizens of the town—the very people whose friends and neighbors were sitting on the jury. History hinges on moments like these common interests.

The trial had begun with a change of venue from Logan County, where the Battle of Blair Mountain was fought, to Jefferson County, near Harpers Ferry, West Virginia. Once the location was set, union organizers approached the businessmen's associations, hotels, and private citizens for help sheltering the

200 miners and their families headed for Charles Town. When they arrived at the train station, wearing pink lapel ribbons identifying them as UMWA defendants, a cheering crowd marched them to the fire station's public hall.

In the lead role, Bill Blizzard, a handsome young man with a lovely spouse and two children along for the trial, maintained a cheerful attitude, as if he were not facing the gallows.

Blizzard's son and biographer, William C. Blizzard, wrote in the book *When Miners March*: "The miners were out to make friends and they passed up few opportunities," and "many of the citizens of Charles Town learned that these supposed revolutionists were, after all, not very different from themselves."

They organized a baseball team and they made a point of attending church with their families in the town.

The miners were good at baseball, Blizzard wrote, but they were careful not to win too many games against the Charles Town citizens. When they did win, the proceeds from the game were donated to a hospital fund.

The first trial brought two dozen of the UMWA organizers into court, and Blizzard was named as the lead defendant. His union attorneys faced prejudice from the first, as the coal companies were allowed to keep secret their evidence and witness list. Blizzard's attorneys also protested the fact that groups of well-armed coal company gunmen were present in the courtroom.

The first prosecution witness, West Virginia Governor Ephraim Morgan, did little to help the coal companies. He admitted (as one newspaper wrote) that "a private government, whose army consists of the notorious 'mine guards,' exists in his state, and that though opposed to it, he is powerless to end it."

Within a few days, people began to sense that the State of West Virginia, rather than the miners, was on trial. "It looks as if the entire machinery of government has been turned over to the coal operators," another newspaper wrote.

While the coal companies tried to tie Blizzard and the organizers directly to the military action that took place on Blair Mountain, a principle witness was undermined when it turned out he was being paid by the coal companies. At one point in the trial, the prosecutor brought out a set of Springfield rifles to demonstrate the firepower of the miners. To show what the miners were up against, union lawyers brought out a diabolically constructed bomb dropped on the miners from a biplane. To boost the drama, the union asked experts to take it apart, there in the courtroom.

Day by day, Sunday by Sunday, and game by game, the jury and townsfolk began to see through the prosecution's portrait of the men as traitors who deserved execution. And as the coal industry's case fell apart, the people of Charles Town increasingly took the miners' side. Near the end of the trial, Blizzard's wife was seen entering the courtroom arm-in-arm with a jury member's wife.

On May 27, 1922, Bill Blizzard and fellow defendants were acquitted. "Cheers resounded throughout the courtroom," wrote William C. Blizzard. "Blizzard's mother, wife and children clung to his neck, while the young defendant, all smiles, shook hands with friends until his hand was sore."

In the end, no one was executed, but not all the other miners were acquitted. Some were sentenced to jail terms, but nearly all were paroled by 1925. And it wasn't all smooth sailing for the UMWA afterwards. Union membership dropped drastically in the 1920s, to the point where some historians maintain that the coal companies won the Battle of Blair Mountain.

Wess Harris, publisher of *When Miners March*, disagrees. "That's just a lot of hogwash," Harris said. "If anything, Blair Mountain was a victory. The twin events of Blair Mountain and the trials (at Charles Town) were the furnaces that forged the miners' steel that got them ready for the 1930s." By then, new federal labor laws began to protect labor organizers.

Unions "struggle and lose, then struggle and win," William C. Blizzard wrote. What people need to understand was that there had always been something wrong with an industry that "produced a mint of wealth and forced its employees to live in poverty."

Treason Trial

Labor leader Bill Blizzard at bat in a baseball game, Charles Town, Jefferson County, 1922. Several members of the United Mine Workers were tried for treason following the Battle of Blair Mountain in Logan County during the Mine Wars. In a change of venue, the first trial was held in Charles Town. During the trial, union members, coal company officials, and journalists played baseball. Incidentally, Blizzard was hit by a bat and injured just after this photo was taken. [William Blizzard Collection]

Union Miners Play Hardball.

This photo and the caption below it are both from *Picturing West Virginia*, published by the State Archives Division. Incredibly, in the State Museum at the capitol, along with this image state historians display an old softball as if it were a relic from that game.

The game ball in the June 16, 1963, edition of the *Charleston Gazette-Mail* is a true baseball which is currently on display with the When Miners March Traveling Museum. And despite what the caption below implies, Blizzard's team never played ball with the men who were trying to hang them!

John L. Lewis: Forty Years of Upset Stomachs
Friend to Coal Miners, Tough Foe to Operators

William C. Blizzard

The following article was originally published in a slightly different form in the Charleston Sunday Gazette-Mail, *June 16, 1963.*

FOR MORE THAN FORTY YEARS, FROM 1919 TO 1960, JOHN L. Lewis upset the stomach of the American public as that public absorbed the newspaper headlines with its breakfast. He not only was a friend of the miners, but during most of that time was the greatest friend the sodium bicarbonate manufacturers ever had.

Since November 1, 1919, when Lewis, as acting president of the United Mine Workers of America, called his first nationwide strike of coal miners, the public has been reading these head-lines: "Government Moves to Stop Lewis"; "Lewis Orders Work Stoppage"; "Lewis Orders Miners Back"; "Lewis Flays Coal Operators"; "Lewis Defies Government Board"; and "Lewis Wins Wage Increase." Such headlines were typical for most of Lewis's forty-year tenure, as jonquils and coal miners came out of the ground together almost every spring.

Since his retirement in January, Lewis has been president emeritus of the UMW, has received an honorary doctorate from West Virginia University, and has been praised and feted by many of his former coal company enemies. The honors and praises may have been more prompted by relief than genuine respect or affection, but Lewis's adversaries had best not relax; for there is no reason to think that John L. Lewis's voice still may not ring strong and clear in UMW affairs, for all his eighty-three years.

During forty years the names of Lewis and the UMW were synonymous. Except for brief internal opposition in the '20s and early '30s, John L. Lewis was the unchallenged leader of the coal diggers of the United States. His long tenure was not the result of chance, although neither was Lewis a tyrant who ruled his coal kingdom without the acquiescence of most of his miners.

That is, within the UMW the big bushy-browed man from Iowa built a machine not unlike any other political machine and used it ruthlessly to perpetuate himself in office. How much the machine was needed may never be known, but on occasion it clipped off heads of opposition leaders like so many dandelions before the moving blade. On the other hand, Lewis was always, in an economic showdown, popular with the miners, and another leader of his stature was not on the scene during his reign.

Lewis has been called the Samson of the miners. As such, he was well aware that his strength lay in his union membership and its support, and that shorn of his miners he was as weak as any other man. He never forgot this, nor did he take chances of being scalped. For the miners every day touched the aorta of the nation, and if they wished temporarily to shut off the life of that nation, they were in a position to do so.

Lewis once explained this to Saul Alinsky, author of *John L. Lewis: An Unauthorized Biography* (Putnam, 1949). "When," said Lewis, "we control the production of coal we hold the vitals of our society right in our hands. I can squeeze, twist, and pull until we get the inevitable victory. . . . Stop coal and you stop steel. Stop steel and you stop autos, and then tires and every part of our economy. Therefore, as a strike progresses, the hostility of the press and the government begins to build up pressure against us; but on the other hand the pressures for profits in steel and autos also develop and increase. The industrialists of autos and steel begin to apply pressure on the coal operators to accede to our demands, so that their own fabulous profits will not be interrupted. Thus we become the immovable anvil, with the operators relying on us being hammered into surrender by the pounding blows of steel, autos (here Lewis laughed), and all other industrial allies, or accomplices, if you will."

In a way, this explanation of basic economic facts is the story of John L. Lewis's life. It takes toughness and durability to be an anvil, and both Lewis and his miners have had those qualities to a superlative degree. The union leader's description of his tactics is an excellent piece of writing, clear, graphic, and accurate. But as the role of coal becomes less in our economy—and it is becoming less—this picture is changing, and a leader like Lewis will not be able so easily to paralyze the economy at will.

Nor will the coal miners be in so strong a bargaining position. But this is not the fault of Lewis, nor was automation in the coal-fields brought on by him. For automation is a trend, with profit-making as its basis, which will ultimately affect every worker in the United States. The coal miner's plight is the prologue to a greater drama.

If you wish to know a great deal about John L. Lewis with minimum effort, you should read Saul Alinsky's book mentioned above. In toto, the book is pro-Lewis, but it has profundity and lacks that reverence and servility which Alinsky describes as "reflected in the unhealthy awe that permeates every cranny and every stone of the UMW building in Washington, from its outside step to the ceiling of the sixth floor, and to that great Holy of Holies, where the union God abides."

No matter what his faults, which basically were arrogance and pride, John L. Lewis was the most able American labor leader of the past half century, and will retain that title until his death. If his great shadow killed off or withered other potential giants, it is the way of the towering oaks of human society just as it is the way of great oaks of the forest.

John Llewellyn Lewis was born in Lucas, Iowa, on February 12 (Lincoln's birthday), 1880, the oldest son of a Welsh coal miner who was a member of the Knights of Labor. His father, Thomas, helped lead a strike in 1882 against the White Breast Fuel Co., a strike which was lost, leading to the blacklisting of Thomas as a union man too dangerous to hire.

Like many another man who has fought city hall in one guise or another, Thomas Lewis found the going hard, traveling from one area to another to secure work, losing jobs as the blacklist caught up with him. But in 1897 the blacklists were destroyed, and the Lewis family moved back to Lucas, where the father and two of his sons, one of them John, worked in the mines.

John L. Lewis never finished the eighth grade. But he liked to read and he liked to debate. Just under six feet and powerfully built, in his teens he organized both a debating team and a baseball team in Lucas. There he also met Myrta Edith Bell, daughter of a doctor from Ohio, of a family with strong cultural traditions. It was Miss Bell, later to become his wife, who encouraged John L. Lewis's love of reading and guided him to the classics which later emerged in his public speeches.

But Lewis was not to marry his childhood sweetheart for some years. At twenty-one he left home and traveled throughout the West, hitching rides on freights when he had to and working in many mines, digging for metal as well as coal. He was gone from Lucas for five years, returning to Iowa and the coal mines in 1906. (Lewis has said: "I suppose if we talk about formal education I would count that five years as my education. It was a very important part of my life.")

By that time he had the basic qualities of a leader: the ability to speak well, a forceful physical appearance, aggressiveness, strong convictions, and ambition. He ran for mayor of Lucas shortly after he married Myrta Bell in 1907 but was defeated. The local miners, however, sent him as a delegate to the national convention of the UMW that year.

Lewis was almost thirty when he moved to Panama, Illinois, largely because he thought he had a better chance to make a showing as a labor leader in that area. Helped by his five brothers, who had also moved to Panama, he soon was elected local union president, then state legislative agent for the district UMW. It was in Illinois, after a pit disaster which killed 160 miners, that Lewis began his long career of separating politicians from their hides in order to gain benefits for the miners. His record before the Illinois Legislature brought Lewis to the attention of AFL President Samuel Gompers.

Gompers at the time needed a strong, tough man who also had brains, and in 1911 hired Lewis as a field representative and legislative agent for the American Federation of Labor. The big man from Lucas now was working as a union lobbyist and AFL organizer in the steel, lumber, glass, rubber, and electrical industries, on a national level. From the age of about thirty-one to thirty-seven, he worked for the AFL, trying to organize the above named industries on a craft basis. He failed.

But he did not fail to advance himself within the UMW, of which he was yet a member, using his AFL position and expense account to build a personal machine within the miner's union. During the 1916 UMW national convention he served as UMW president pro tempore, and shortly afterward took a job as chief statistician for the UMW, resigning his AFL job.

Lewis had not failed to see the strategic role of the coal industry in the nation, and his failure to organize industries on a craft basis had taught him the value in mass industries, of the industrial union approach of the UMW. In 1916, John L. Lewis moved with his family to Indianapolis, which was then national UMW headquarters.

Lewis was on his way, but not even he could have anticipated how fast he was destined to move. In 1917, John P. White, seventh president of the UMW, resigned and was succeeded by Frank Hayes, who appointed Lewis vice president. Hayes had little interest in union affairs, liked the cup that cheers, and was mild-mannered and unaggressive.

Lewis, it may be safely said, was neither mild nor unaggressive, and the UMW, as he could plainly see, was to be his life. Under Frank Hayes, he actually ran the UMW show, and in 1919 presided over the UMW national convention. In 1920, at the age of forty, he was elected president of the miners' union, a post he held for forty years, or ten years longer than the combined service of the eight UMW presidents who had preceded him.

John L. Lewis had arrived. Only ten years before, or a little better, he had been a mere local union president at Panama, Illinois.

Lewis was to call a nationwide strike, however, before he officially became the UMW chief. The war was over, and in the fall of 1919 there were nearly 400,000 members in the UMW. World War I had produced the usual crop of war-making millionaires, while the coal miners had worked for $5 a day, pledged not only to not strike, but also to not ask for any change in wages or working conditions for the duration.

In 1919, with the war ended, UMW acting president Lewis called a strike for higher wages, a shorter work week, and a six-hour day, to begin November 1, 1919. The government insisted that the war was technically still on, although shooting had stopped a year before, and Woodrow Wilson, an enemy of labor, forbade the strike.

The miners went out November 1 just the same, defying a federal court injunction. Lewis and eighty-four union officials were cited for contempt. On December 7, Lewis called off the strike, defeated by Woodrow Wilson and the federal courts. But the miners did receive an immediate small increase through

Lewis's agreement with Wilson, and another larger increase from an appointed commission a little later.

John L. Lewis had led his first national strike, and all had not gone so well. There is evidence that the coal miners were considerably more militant than their chief at that time, and that the UMW convention which greeted Lewis after he called off the strike was hostile. The convention ratified his actions and agreement only by the use of the existing, but yet weak, Lewis machine.

Lewis learned much from the 1919 struggle, the principal lesson being that it was both uncomfortable and inconvenient to face a large room full of hostile coal miners who could, if sufficiently aroused, fire you from your job. Lewis determined to see to it that the UMW became a unified force which would back his orders and give him job security. That is, he built a machine, a good heavy one that would iron out threats to his rule.

At the same time that such a machine secured Lewis's personal position, it also insured that 400,000 coal miners would act as a unit, so that their strength might be felt. Lewis looked upon himself as a commander in chief, and he knew that only with a disciplined army could victories be won. The army of miners became an extension of his will, just as any army is the extension and implement of the will of any general. It remained that for forty years.

He assured his control of the UMW by revoking autonomy in the union districts in the coal states. That is, top UMW district officials were elected by their membership before the Lewis reign, but were appointed by Lewis not many years after he took office. If they supported his policies, he retained them; if they opposed him, he fired them, replacing them with his own men. The Lewis men heading the districts then enforced Lewis policies in their respective areas.

This was not, in some cases, easily done, but done it was. Lewis ran against Sam Gompers in 1921 for presidency of the AFL but was beaten two to one when the votes were counted. Some UMW district leaders who didn't like Lewis helped in his defeat and also fought his national UMW leadership.

Principal among them were Frank Farrington of Illinois and Alex Howat of Kansas. Charles A. Madison, in *American Labor Leaders* (Harper, 1950), states flatly that when John Brophy, president of UMW District 2 in Pennsylvania, ran against Lewis for the UMW presidency in 1926, he was "counted out by machine tactics." (Many years later, however, Lewis appointed Brophy to the post of executive director of the newborn CIO.)

Lewis's tactics at UMW conventions are described by Saul Alinsky:

> At one of the conventions, Alex Howat made his customary Pickett's charge down the center aisle and up onto the platform. Then came the usual aftermath as Howat was seized and sent sailing through the air and into the audience and Lewis's followers on the platform panted from the exertion necessary from this feat. Howat's demands for recognition by Chairman Lewis were denied and the convention began to shout and hiss and boo its disapproval. Lewis calmly regarded the bedlam for some moments and then boomed, "May the chair state that you may shout until you meet each other in hell and he will not change his ruling."

There were socialists and Communists in the UMW at that time, and Lewis disliked them as much as they disliked him. He had prepared a series of articles on the Red menace, at UMW expense, which were widely circulated in newspapers and magazines. In the articles, he asserted, in essence, that all radicals and many liberals were agents of Moscow, and that many UMW troubles arose from their treasonous activity.

In his effort to defeat all comers, Lewis pulled out all stops and used all tactics which he hoped might be effective. The ethics of the matter were seldom, if ever, considered, just as they seldom are by practical and ambitious men in any line of endeavor. The criterion of any tactic apparently was "Will it work?"

Using this same criterion, for instance, Lewis in his CIO days (1935–40), forgot his former hatred of leftists. During the early days of the CIO, Lewis needed help in the organization of mass industries. He needed organizers who were intelligent, fearless, and possessed of missionary zeal. Among Communists and other radicals he found these qualities, and he did not hesitate to hire them. John Brophy and Powers Hapgood, for instance, were hired and placed in top positions in the CIO. Neither was a Communist, but both were critics of capitalism and favored some sort of socialist society.

In addition, both had fought Lewis in the UMW, and sharp blows had been exchanged. Nevertheless, Lewis hired them to rock the cradle of his brainchild, the CIO, and they proved able babysitters, in more ways than one, as Goodyear and General Motors were to learn. All along the line Lewis hired CIO personnel who could do the job best, and did not, as he put it, "turn them upside down to see what sort of literature fell out of their pockets."

Such radicals spearheaded the CIO drive, although it should be emphasized that they in no way originated or managed the CIO. That responsibility belonged to Lewis. The fact that most of them were later ejected from that organization is the sort of irony that history seems fond of.

The early years of Lewis leadership were not happy ones for the UMW, which shrank from a membership of more than 425,000 in 1921 to less than 150,000 in 1932. Part of this may have been Lewis's fault, as his critics claimed, but much of this withering was caused by the economics of the coal industry, plus the economic and political power of big business prior to 1929.

Coal was so plentiful that what the coal miner was bringing to the surface was not bringing much of a price. There were too many coal mines and coal miners, all fiercely competing with one another, supplying too much coal to a glutted market. A union leader does not, under such conditions, find it easy or even possible to keep wages rising, and if a union does not do that its membership drifts away.

The debacle of 1929 made matters worse. Then came the U.S. election year of 1932, with Herbert Hoover opposing Franklin D. Roosevelt. Lewis favored Hoover, partly because the Norris-LaGuardia Act was passed during his tenure, and in part possibly because of early bias toward the Republican Party. But when Roosevelt took office, and Lewis was able to get Section 7A of the National Industry Recovery Act into law, the mine union leader immediately supported Roosevelt.

This famous Section 7A, which affirmed the right of workers to join a union of their choice, was the work of John L. Lewis, and led to the rebirth of the UMW in the early '30s and the founding and success of the CIO.

John L. Lewis has fought hard for both Republican and Democratic candidates, but he explained his political beliefs at the National Press Club in 1936: "I am not a Republican. I am not a Democrat. I am not a Fascist, Communist, or a Socialist."

What political party, you might ask, does this leave? It leaves none, actually, for Lewis has always been for the politician who was for him, for the UMW, and for labor, and he felt that all three of these were a united trinity. This has been the key to Lewis's politics, although he seldom found a politician in that category.

If a politician really wasn't in that category, however, Lewis often made a counterfeit labor sympathizer do just as well. And

there were lots of them. Franklin Roosevelt was such a counterfeit, according to Lewis.

According to Lewis, Roosevelt actually fought the enactment
of Section 7A. But Lewis did not tell the coal miners of this
Roosevelt attitude, and he knew FDR was publicly proclaiming
sympathy for labor. So Lewis sent his organizers into the coalfields, pointing to Section 7A and saying: "President Roosevelt
wants you to join the union!"

Roosevelt, of course, had said no such thing, but Lewis knew
that FDR, for political reasons, was not likely to deny it. By
late 1933, UMW membership had risen to more than 500,000,
and the CIO was a gleam in John L. Lewis's eye. He argued the
merits of industrial versus craft unionism with top AFL leaders,
but met a stone wall. Although William Green had been a coal
miner and secretary-treasurer of the UMW at one time, and
was yet a UMW member, he and his executive council in 1935
turned down the Lewis offer to help "organize the unorganized."
(Saul Alinsky credits this slogan to Lewis, but it was coined by
John Brophy, or at least appeared in print under his byline, as
early as 1926.)

Then Lewis and the heads of seven AFL craft unions met
and formed the Committee (later the Congress) for Industrial
Organization. Lewis himself was still an AFL vice president but
resigned his post in late 1935. In August 1936, the AFL ejected the
CIO unions, charging dual unionism. The UMW also was ejected,
and Lewis retaliated by ousting William Green from his original
union.

There is no space here to detail the CIO organizing drive in
rubber, steel, and other industries. Lewis gave about three-quar-
ters of a million dollars to the second Roosevelt campaign, and
FDR captured all but eight of the nation's 531 electoral votes. But
in 1937, during the General Motors "sit-down" strike, Lewis began to mistrust Roosevelt, who apparently told the labor leader

he favored the sit-downs, and Michigan governor Frank Murphy just the opposite.

Lewis expected a friendly Roosevelt because of the large amount of money donated to his 1936 campaign. And Lewis became convinced that not only was Roosevelt unfriendly, but he was stabbing him in the back. When he discovered, through Frank Murphy, that Roosevelt had his telephones tapped by the FBI at his office and at home, and that he was under surveillance by J. Edgar Hoover, Lewis was understandably miffed.

On October 25, 1940, the UMW head made his famous radio speech in which he opposed Roosevelt for reelection and threatened to resign from the CIO if FDR were elected. Roosevelt was elected for a third term, and Lewis kept his word. That this was a tragedy for the CIO, the UMW, and the entire labor movement seems, with hindsight, painfully evident.

Some of Lewis's old UMW cohorts, like Van Bittner and Phillip Murray, broke with Lewis or were booted by him from the UMW when they persisted in supporting Roosevelt. In October 1941, Lewis took the UMW from the CIO. The latter organization split into warring factions within a few years, then united with the AFL. Lewis went back into the AFL for a time but took his miners out again. Today, as has been true for several years, the labor movement is badly divided, snubbed by politicians and hamstrung by the Taft-Hartley Act and other restrictive legislation.

It is true that for some years Lewis had considered the establishment of a third major political party with a farmer-laborer base. But he knew that such a party could succeed, possibly by taking over the Democratic Party, only with the support of an organized, unified labor movement. If Lewis had remained with the CIO, such a huge, unified movement might have been possible under his leadership. That a third party was not possible without a mighty labor base was demonstrated by the Progressive Party fiasco in 1948.

But, as Lewis has pointed out, speculation on what might have been is futile. He went on to fight Roosevelt during the war against Germany and Japan, in 1943 calling out his miners three times (after a preliminary spontaneous walkout) in protest against the "little steel formula," which had the effect of freezing wages. Lewis won increases for the miners including the Welfare and Retirement Fund, but he also reaped vilification on an unprecedented scale.

Lewis was cursed by the left, the right, and the man on the street for striking his miners during World War II. But he knew what he was doing from a tactical point of view, and the coal miners followed his orders in an impressive show of solidarity and loyalty. They were fighting a sort of war underground, and it is interesting to know that the coal miners in the course of their work from 1941 through 1945 lost 6,561 killed and 322,873 wounded.

In the years before his retirement, Lewis concentrated upon improving the miners' Welfare and Retirement Fund, until the royalty that financed it reached forty cents a ton, and he built ten hospitals in West Virginia and Kentucky. From a public relations and humanitarian point of view, nothing he ever did surpassed this program.

What Lewis had done for his miners in other ways, however, was not only impressive but almost incredible. During the period 1935 to 1939, among fifteen major basic industries the average wage of coal miners was third from the bottom. Ten years later, Lewis had increased that wage by 246.8 percent, and wages of coal miners led all the rest.

Lewis retired from the UMW leadership in 1960 and is now the union's president emeritus. Whether another Lewis is now developing to cope with modern problems is unknown, but none is now visible. There are problems. Automation has reduced coal mine employees to about 136,000, and the Welfare

Fund is threatened. Four of the union hospitals may be forced to close.

John L. Lewis was and is a complex man, and the final story about him and his role in the labor movement has not been written. But the importance of his role is not to be doubted. Perhaps it is well that the Samson of labor is stepping out of the picture at a time when his strength is being shorn away by automation.

Whatever the verdict of history, another such man is not likely soon to appear on the national scene.

> "If we must grind up human flesh and bone in the industrial machine that we call modern America, then before God, I assert that those who consume the coal, and you and I who benefit from that service because we live in comfort, we owe protection to those men first, and we owe the security for their family if they die. I say it, I voice it, I proclaim it, and I care not who in heaven or hell opposes it!"
>
> —John Llewellyn Lewis
> February 12, 1880–June 11, 1969

An Open Letter

Cecil Roberts to Randall Reid-Smith

United Mine Workers of America

CECIL E. ROBERTS
INTERNATIONAL PRESIDENT

TELEPHONE
(703) 291-2420
FAX (703) 291-2451

UNITED MINE WORKERS' HEADQUARTERS
18354 QUANTICO GATEWAY DRIVE, SUITE 200
Triangle, VA
22172-1779

July 26, 2011

Mr. Randall Reid-Smith, Commissioner
WV Division of Culture and History
The Culture Center
1900 Kanawha Blvd., East
Charleston, WV 25305

Dear Mr. Reid-Smith,

Shortly after the opening of the West Virginia State Museum, it was brought to my attention that there are a series of inaccuracies in the description of the UMWA, UMWA personnel and coal miners' history in the museum's displays. Additionally, I have received many complaints about the overall impression a visitor receives of the UMWA's role in West Virginia's history, life in the company towns, the events leading up to the Battle of Blair Mountain, the battle itself and other aspects of the displays in the museum.

Over the past months, several members of the UMWA staff have visited the West Virginia State Museum on many separate occasions. I have been to the museum myself, and seen the displays there. I have a number of very serious concerns with what is an inaccurate portrayal of the UMWA and our history of oppression and struggle against the coal operators of the 19th and 20th centuries.

The UMWA's concerns with the museum's displays are not only about the factual inaccuracies, but also extend to numerous misleading statements and lack of full information provided in the exhibits.

Let me start with this: There are two completely inaccurate statements in the museum's displays that I would like to see changed immediately:

- On "The Failure of Violence" plaque, the museum's text says that Bill Blizzard became the President of "Local" 17 of the UMWA. In fact, he became President of District 17, not Local 17. A local union is operational at only one workplace. A District encompasses all the local unions within a geographical area, in this case, southern West Virginia.

- On the "Bill Blizzard" plaque, the same mistake is made. Raymond Lewis became District 17 President, not Local 17. We also have concerns about the statement that Bill Blizzard resigned because John L. Lewis demoted him solely in order to put his brother in Blizzard's place.

Beyond these outright mistakes, there are a host of misleading statements, biases, and incomplete information in almost every exhibition concerning coal miners, life in the coal camps, and more.

Specifically, the following "rooms" in the museum contain displays that are objectionable and do not present the actual history of these things anywhere near what it actually was:

- The "Company Store," including the discussion of the system of using mine company scrip instead of U.S. legal tender to pay miners. Your presentation makes it seem as if the scrip system was little different from a credit card, where miners and their families could pay off expensive purchases over time.

Nowhere is it mentioned that miners had absolutely no choice as to whether they used scrip or not. Nowhere is it mentioned that going somewhere else instead of the company store to purchase goods and equipment was an offense frequently punishable by a beating from the company's Baldwin-Felts thugs followed by dismissal from employment and eviction from the company house.

- "Coal mining," including misleading statements regarding Island Creek Coal and UMWA organizing, as well as a very small presentation regarding the worst industrial disaster in United States history – the explosion at the Monongah mine – that includes language regarding the company's Christmas "gift" to the families of those killed that is offensive to the memories of the fallen miners.

- "The Battle of Blair Mountain," which blames Sid Hatfield for instigating the violence in the coalfields that led to that battle, instead of focusing on the daily violence inflicted on coal miners and their families in the coal camps of the day.

The film you show about Blair Mountain and accompanying panels also say that Bill Blizzard and others who were tried in the aftermath of the Battle were charged with treason against the United States, when in fact they were charged with treason against the state of West Virginia. As I'm sure you know, one cannot be treasonous against a single state, one can only be treasonous against all the United States. You fail to point this out, thereby perpetuating the false notion that these men were not true Americans.

There are several other issues with these and other displays that the UMWA finds objectionable, misleading, and biased; and which we are willing to discuss with you and your staff.

It is, to say the least, disappointing to find that what is supposed to be an authoritative presentation on our state's unique history – and one that surely costs West Virginia taxpayers millions of dollars to build and maintain – contains inaccurate, false, misleading and biased presentations.

Indeed, in just about every instance where the UWMA is mentioned in the museum, we are linked with violence or some other unsavory activity. There is no mention of the millions of West Virginians who have, over the past 60+ years, received and continue to receive the benefits of UMWA pensions and retiree health care – considerably easing their senior years – which were negotiated by the UMWA.

There is no mention of the UMWA's leading role in passing mine safety and health legislation which have saved countless lives in West Virginia and throughout the nation. There is no mention of the UMWA's role in fighting to end black lung and to establish and then protect black lung compensation.

Instead, the impression a visitor with little or no knowledge of the history of the coal industry and the UMWA would take away from the museum is that the union is made up of people who, while perhaps willing to work hard, are just as willing to be prone to armed violence to settle our problems, be they internal or external.

It is said that the "victors write history." I would point out that the fight between coal miners, our families and our communities against those who would exploit us is far from over. We have no intention of allowing a twisted version of what life was really like for our ancestors and ourselves to be foisted on an unsuspecting public.

I look forward to hearing from you as to how soon you intend to correct the false information contained in the museum, and whether or not you intend to work with the UMWA on correcting the biases imparted by so many of the museum's displays.

Sincerely,

Cecil E. Roberts

Cecil E. Roberts

cc: Hon. Earl Ray Tomblin, Governor
Hon. Jay Rockefeller, United States Senator
Hon. Nick Rahall, Member of Congress
Hon. Kay Huffman Goodwin, Secretary, Department of Education and the Arts
Hon. Jeffrey Kessler, Acting President of the Senate
Hon. Rick Thompson, Speaker of the House
Hon. Mike Caputo, Majority Whip
Joe Carter, UMWA International District 17 Vice President
Gary Trout, UMWA Region IV Director
Ted Hapney, UMWA Eastern COMPAC Director
Marty Hudson, Executive Assistant to the UMWA President
Bob Scaramozzino, Administrator, UMWA President's Office
Phil Smith, UMWA Director of Communications
Emily Smith, UMWA Archivist/Collection Manager
Paul Nyden, Charleston Gazette
Ken Ward, Charleston Gazette

Cecil Roberts Shares His Story
Michael Kline

I READ AND REREAD THE WORDS OF CECIL ROBERTS WITH blurred excitement. The idea that the leader of the United Mine Workers would go public with his critique of the *Coal* exhibit at the West Virginia State Museum gave me hope. In the current political climate in Charleston, our governors, judges, and legislative leaders still dance to the beat of Don Blankenship's drum. "We are the extractive state," they proclaim, "and we are open for business." Never mind that the major proceeds of this business are leaving the state. The profits go elsewhere and always have, leaving our citizens deprived and demoralized. In this oppressive atmosphere of intense lobbying and rising corporate profits we have seen few signs of hope on the horizon, hope for more recognition of the lives our forebears lived under the whiplash of company rule, hope for an unveiling of a more accurate accounting of our industrial culture and union organizing history than as it is currently portrayed in State exhibits and publications. The Roberts letter above is one of those signs. It is a sign that authentic interpretations of coalfield life and memory will prevail, despite apparent sustained efforts to suppress and sanitize them. Our grandchildren will take an interest in how the "grands" came through it all. They will stand a little taller.

In the early fall of 2011, President Roberts agreed to sit for a recorded interview exploring issues of labor history in the arenas of public culture and history. We met at the headquarters of the United Mine Workers of America in Triangle, Virginia. Carrie Kline joined me in this documentary opportunity as did Phil Smith, director of communications for the Union. The Headquarters' hallways are hung with haunting and historically significant photos alongside glass cases laden with artifacts and documents tracing early developments in Union history. We could have spent days trying to absorb this extensive exhibit. Here is an organization that has gone to great lengths to preserve and present its past with vivid accessibility. Our brief tour before the interview felt like an invitation to come inside the story. Once seated with Roberts around a table in the executive office, we could not imagine what sort of a story it would be. But we always begin our interviews with the same question.

Michael Kline: Tell me about your people and where you were raised.

Cecil Roberts: I was born in Kayford, West Virginia. You go fifteen miles up Cabin Creek Road and then the black top runs out. And then you turn to the right on a dirt road called Shamrock Hollow. And I was born in a company house there in 1946 and delivered by a company doctor and in the company house. We were all raised in the company house, company town, lived there on Cabin Creek all my life until I was elected to come here. I went straight from Cabin Creek to Washington, DC, which is a little bit of a difference (laughs) in culture, among other things, yes.

You might be amazed by how many people lived in Kayford at that time. People used to actually fight over . . . When someone moved out of a company house, and people knew someone was moving, you'd go to the company store and you'd sign a list and say, "I want to be considered for Phil Smith's house when he moves out." But the superintendent of the company store made that determination of who got to live in what house.

Everywhere you looked there was a house, and there wasn't an empty house to be seen anywhere back up in those hollows. All the company houses I lived in weren't identical, but they were very close to it.

Coal mining in those days was—this is before mechanization had really taken a stronghold—miners were mostly hand-loading back in the '40s and '50s. And my earliest recollection is that coal miners were everywhere.

Mechanization

Roberts: The UMWA was the largest union in the country in the '30s. We were over 800,000 members, and that held true for a while. And then mechanization came along. The first wave of mechanization was probably around the early '50s. There had been some of that in the late '40s, but it really hit hard in the '50s when [UMWA President] John L. Lewis pretty much accepted mechanization, that it was inevitable. You weren't going to stop companies from being able to mine coal with loading machines, and cutting machines, shuttle cars. And so a lot of people lost their jobs. They were hand-loaders. The UMWA sometime in the early '50s lost like 300,000 members, all in a matter of a few years after signing the contract that created the Health and Retirement Funds in the late '40s. So by the time I was born, the Union was changing dramatically, coal mining was changing dramatically, and it really changed by the mid-'50s, and in a very profound way.

I guess we saw the first wave of real unemployment hit hard in the coalfields in those days. A lot of people left the coalfields and made their way to places like Cleveland, Ohio, Detroit, Michigan, and Flint, Michigan, to go to work in the auto factories, and the steel mills of Pittsburgh, and other places. So a lot of people migrated from West Virginia and Kentucky out of the coalfields to other areas of the country. That's why you find so many people who tell you, "My grandfather was a coal miner or my great-grandfather." That is all true because we had 800,000 people mining coal in 1938, '39, '40 and down to probably 500,000 mining coal by the mid-'50s. So where did all those people go? Well, they left and they took their kids with them and most of them had four, five, six kids. Some of them had ten kids, and then *they* all had kids. And you hear those stories wherever you go. My recollection is that when we got into the '60s, we began to see lots of layoffs, not because of mechanization per se, but because the demand for coal was down. From about 1960 up until about 1970 almost no one was hired in the coal industry. If people were working in the coal industry in 1960, they might have had jobs throughout the '60s, but there wasn't this mass attempt to hire people.

More Changes

Roberts: Of course, that changed in 1970, '71. If you remember around the time of the 1973 Arab oil embargo, literally thousands of young people were hired in the industry. And I was one of them. Those people who were hired were a little different. I was a Vietnam veteran. Lots of Vietnam veterans were hired. Many of those young people who went in the mines with me had some college backgrounds. Some had a little more extensive education than perhaps those who were working in the mines at that time. So you had this great conflict between the older miners who were in their fifties and younger miners in their twenties. Two different kinds of thinking about the way things ought to be done. When a foreman would ask a young person to do something that he thought was dangerous, he's not doing it. And then you had a lot of wildcat strikes, a lot of turmoil about that same time. And we had the Farmington disaster in 1968. Tony Boyle went down after the Farmington disaster and praised the company. And they had just had an explosion that killed seventy-eight men. So you had all those things that came together. This was not only in the coal industry but within the Union itself. Down in the southern part of the state the black lung movement was ongoing. It was very much a rank-and-file movement. You had a handful of doctors, maybe a couple of lawyers supporting that effort.

The Union for the most part wasn't supporting that. And you had this clash between the rank and file and the establishment in the Union led by Tony Boyle and others. On the other hand, you had this effort by Jock Yablonski, who had run [for the presidency of the Union] on a platform of autonomy and democracy. He lost the election and then lost his life. And then you had Miners for Democracy, so you had all that turmoil within the Union coming between 1968 and 1972. That was about the most significant four years that I can point to as far as changes within the movement itself, yet when Arnold Miller got elected he brought democracy to the Union and people like me had an opportunity to run for office. And if it wasn't for Jock Yablonski and Arnold Miller, maybe I wouldn't be sitting here talking to you. I might be pumping gas somewhere down around Chelyan or Cabin Creek or somewhere. But they opened doors and many of us were ready to walk through. That would include Rich Trumka, myself, and many other young people at that time. We took advantage of the autonomy and ran for office and got elected.

Farmington Blood Brings New Laws

Roberts: So, within those four years, you had a passage of the first federal legislation to protect coal miners: 1969 Coal Mine Health and Safety Act, which included for the first time the recognition of pneumoconiosis as an occupational disease. And with the explosion at Farmington [came a new level of public awareness], with people watching on television—not just in the coalfields but in Los Angeles, Florida, New York City—watching the mine explode and then explode again, watching interviews with the widows. I think television might have played a huge role in bringing about the federal legislation to protect coal miners, because it was not just something confined to Cabin Creek and Paint Creek and places like that. It was like the whole nation watched. So I've always said that the seventy-eighty miners who lost their lives in Farmington were kind of like heroes on a battlefield, that they gave their lives for everyone else.

If you look at statistics of the 1969 Coal Mine Health and Safety Act, forty years before the passage of the act, 30,000 miners lost their lives mining coal in the nation. Forty years afterwards, it was less than 3,000. The passage of that act saved many lives. I think the tragedy of this is that we didn't pass this legislation sooner. We've had worse coal mine accidents and explosions. You had Centralia in Illinois, where hundreds lost their lives. Nothing happened. It was in the early '50s. You had another explosion at West Frankfort, and over 100 miners lost their lives. Nothing happened legislatively. It took a tragedy like Farmington that everyone watched for the changes to come about.

The Black Lung Toll

Roberts: Then you think about the hundreds of thousands of people who suffered from pneumoconiosis and never received benefits or even had the fact [established] that such disease existed. [The year] 1969 was the first time the country acknowledged that pneumoconiosis was an occupational illness. I think that's tragic in and of itself. So I think 1968 to 1972 is a significant time. You can look backward from there, and you can look forward from there to see how coal mining has been dealt with. I mean, it took, I guess, close to a hundred years [after the birth of the coal mining industry] to have health and safety laws passed by the Congress, and it took the same amount of time to recognize black lung as a disease. Miners used to call it "miner's asthma." They knew they were sick and they figured they got sick from mining coal, but no one could tell them, or would tell them, what was wrong with them. Miners used to choke to death and never be compensated a dime for it. Miners died at a very young age.

So one of the tragedies, I think, of the coalfields is a failure to protect miners until very recently. We went the vast majority of the time without any protection for coal miners either healthwise or safetywise. There's been over 100,000 coal miners killed in this nation's mines. In addition over 100,000 have died from black lung. So we've got over 200,000 miners who lost their lives and most of those lives have been lost without any protection from the government. And I think that's one of the sad stories of coal mining in the United States of America.

But I guess the good news is that we did pass legislation in 1969. We built on that. And miners mining today are safer. They mine coal with a longwall as opposed to a shovel. Mining is not quite the backbreaking work it once was. And we have recognized black lung as an occupational illness, although I do think it is tragic that we don't compensate more miners than we do. I mean, probably around 12 to 14 percent of those people who apply for the benefits now receive them. Not long ago, it was only 7 percent receiving benefits. But every miner walking in applying for black lung benefits a few years back would get them. So there is a tragic story here about health and safety that we all can look back on and talk about how we could've done things a lot better.

Two Houses for $100

Roberts: Then we can spin backward to the period of my youth, from my birth in 1946 to 1969. And using that as a benchmark, for the most part, up until the '60s coal miners were still living in coal company houses and still going to the company store. And there is no shame in moving into a—. I never saw anything wrong with living in a company house, but I think the fact that miners didn't have the flexibility to buy their own homes is something to speak to here. My dad built our house. He bought a property back in the '50s and then over a three-year period built his own home on Cabin Creek at a place called Dawes. My mom and dad would get their mail in Miami on Cabin Creek, so we were kind of right on the border of Miami and Dawes. We had to move from a company house at Kayford to a company house at Acme because they were putting in an overhead belt line over the top of the houses where we lived in Kayford. And then they sold us our house for $50 and we bought the house next to us for $50. So Daddy bought two houses for $100 but we had to tear them down and move them out. He took materials from the two houses we bought to build the house that my mother lives in now. You can go down the basement and see the old black two-by-twelves Dad used for the subflooring. You can go up in the attic and see the old two-by-fours. And they're real dark and rough cut. But we took the lumber out of those two company houses to build the house at Dawes, and I helped him tear those houses down. I was about eleven years old then and helped him some with the building. It took him about three years. He built that house by hand with the help of his brother, my uncle. And an old, retired carpenter lived close by; he'd come over and help. That house has a special place for all of us because Daddy built it with his hands.

Kline: And he was working in mines all of this time?

Roberts: Yes, he was.

Kline: What was his name?

Roberts: Same as mine. Cecil Roberts. I think Dad might have been about sixteen when he started work in the mines. He went in with my grandfather. I never met either one of my grandfathers. They were both killed in the mines before I was born. Dad's father's name was Robert Roberts and he took Dad in the mines with him. And then when he was killed, Daddy kind of became the head of the household. He had two younger brothers at home and he had to help to raise them, help my grandmother. And then my grandfather on my mother's side, he also was killed in the mines. Both of them were killed by slate falls on Cabin Creek. So I've never had the benefit of grandfathers to talk to or hear stories from. And like I said, they both were killed in mines.

Best Health Care in the World

Roberts: The mines, you know, the mines have taken a lot of good men over many, many years. Of course, miners have made really good wages and benefits over the years and had excellent health care for the most of their lives as a result of what Lewis did in 1946 and '47. Pension plans have been fairly decent. It's not provided benefits to miners at a level that they could—until recently—support their families on once they retired. We've done pretty well in the last ten or fifteen years with respect to that. We've been able to raise benefits for miners who retired recently. But we take great pride in the fact that we have some of the best health care in the world and have had that since 1946. And it's been a fight to keep it, but we're proud that we still have it.

So it's been a lot of pain and suffering in the coalfields. And the fact that when people get killed one or two at time it doesn't draw the attention that a Sago or an Upper Big Branch might receive, or with respect to Farmington. But more miners have been killed one or two at a time than at (much larger disasters). A lot of miners have been killed by slate falls, maybe electrocuted, run over by equipment, and those tragedies are just as painful and hurtful to families as those that grab the news and receive all the attention on TV. Those families hurt just as bad as the other families hurt. A lot of tragedies and a lot of pain and suffering goes with coal mining, but it is an honorable profession. I'm proud that I came from a coal mining family and proud that I'm a coal miner myself.

School Days: Good Times, Hard Times

Kline: Can you talk about what it was like to be a kid growing up at that time and your schooling?

Roberts: Sure. I went to the Kayford Elementary School. It doesn't exist anymore, but I went there until I was in the third grade. That's when we moved down to Acme. I went from the third grade to the sixth grade at Acme Elementary School. A minister there from one of the Methodist churches, Cecil Burns, was the principal at Acme. I still remember him very well. I remember going to the Kayford Company Store to shop, and in fact was probably the one that painted the store the last time it was painted, when I was seventeen years of age. That was my first job, painting some company stores when I was seventeen. I got very wealthy doing it, $1.25 an hour, I think that's what I was getting for it. That was minimum wage back in those days. I went to school every day, had good friends and good teachers.

I guess some people might look at us and say we were poor, but I didn't know that. I mean, you just know what surrounds you, right?

Kline: And your playmates, the kids that you knew around Cabin Creek? They were all pretty healthy?

Roberts: Yes, all the kids that I played with were coal miners' sons and daughters. People forget how many folks lived in those coal camps back then.

We never wanted for anything even when Dad would be laid off in the '60s. A lot of layoffs occurred in the late '50s and throughout the '60s. Dad was unemployed for about three years in the coalfields. And he left and went to Ohio to work for a while, then he came back and got a job in the mines again on Cabin

Creek. So we had times when Dad was not working very regularly. That was tough.

Kline: Did you go to Ohio with him at that point?

Roberts: No, Mom and the kids stayed home. And Dad stayed with his brother and worked at building these huge shovels in one of the factories out in, I think, Marion, Ohio. And he was, like I said, he was in and out for about three years. He'd come home or we'd go out to see him. We'd go out there at Christmastime or whatever so we could stay together. And then when he had a chance to get a job back in the mines, he took it. And Dad was able to work up until the time Bethlehem Steel shut down at Kayford. And I think they announced the closure in '79. He worked there up until about March of 1980. And I thought Dad would never enjoy retirement, but I don't think anyone ever enjoyed retirement more than he did.

Kline: What do you mean?

Roberts: Well, he just, you know, he was always on the midnight shift. So Dad would sleep during the day. He was a Union fire boss. So he had to go out to work early in order to inspect a mine before anyone else would go in. And he worked, worked, worked, worked, and slept in the daytime when he was in the mines. And then I thought, oh gee, he'll never enjoy retirement. All he's ever done is work. But he enjoyed it once he retired. He and my mother would spend time together. They'd go down—. Everywhere my mother went, Dad went. Mom used to joke about that and said, "Your Dad never went anywhere with me, but now I can't go anywhere without him." And then they'd go to eat, go to shop, and do things together. They were married sixty-eight years. And I used to joke with Dad. I talked to them both at the same time on the phone. On their anniversary I'd say, "Dad, I think this is going to work out." And he said, "I don't know if it is or not." (Laughs) He was joking. He had a great sense of humor. He was a great storyteller. My dad remembered that—. He could tell you about when he was five years old. He remembered that Blair Mountain March. Oh, yeah.

Kline: What did he say about that?

Roberts: He said that all the men were gone and only the women and kids were left. And they, I think they might have been living in a tent at that time over on Seng Creek. And he said everyone was scared to death because they didn't know if their husbands or fathers were coming back or not. They knew the men were marching to Logan. He remembered. He used to tell this as though it happened yesterday. He said, "We were all standing. All the women were gathered up talking and had all of their kids close by. There wasn't a man anywhere unless he was a really old, old person. And about that time, those airplanes flew over. They were going to bomb the miners." You never saw an airplane in 1921, right? Dad said that everyone just looked up like this, spellbound, standing just like frozen there, looking at those planes. Then all once one of the women said, "They're going to bomb us!"—just like that, and panic struck everyone. Dad said my grandmother grabbed him under one arm and my uncle Arnold under another—my Uncle Arnold would have been about three then—started running, and ran into a tent, shoved them under the bed, crawled under the bed with them until the airplanes were gone. And the history is that they did drop bombs, but not on these family members. They dropped them on the miners trying to get to Blair Mountain. The pilots were throwing bombs over the side of the planes. And the woman who screamed out, "They're going to bomb us!" was right. She just didn't know who. And Dad told us the story so eloquently, as though it happened the day before. My dad never lost one bit of mental faculties until he died. And same with my mother. She is ninety-two. Sharp as a tack. Both of them. I've been very much blessed with respect to that.

Cousin Murdered

Roberts: My dad told another story. This was when he was five years old, too. They were living in Seng Creek at that time. I don't know if you know where Seng Creek is. From Kayford, you go through what used to be the tunnel. On the other side of the tunnel, that's called Seng Creek as you went down off the mountain on that road leading into Whitesville on the Boone County side. They were living there. And my grandfather's cousin and one of the Baldwin-Felts guards started having trouble and obviously did not like each other at all.

Kline: Baldwin-Felts?

Roberts: Yeah, guards. Some people called them thugs, but they were out of [a security agency] in Bluefield. You know, they were notorious. They were around for most of the strikes in West Virginia, but starting back in 1912, 1913 on Paint Creek and Cabin Creek, they were pretty much agents of the company, similar to some of the former detective agencies that were formed to break strikes in other industries. If you saw the movie *Matewan*, those were Baldwin-Felts guards that Sid Hatfield killed in the streets there. So you had these guards to do the company's bidding. Grandfather was very much Union and I guess his relatives were all Union too. But my grandfather's cousin was having trouble back and forth with this Baldwin-Felts guard. And they had a large, two-story building there. Downstairs was a bar. Upstairs was an old silent movie theater. To get to the theater you walked up the steps on the side of the building. The Baldwin-Felts guard—this was the middle of day—was at the bar drinking. And he saw my grandfather's cousin walking up those steps. He went outside and killed him, and as he walked up the steps shot him about five times. And our cousin rolled down the steps.

In those days, they didn't have funeral homes. So what did you do with someone that's dead? Well, they brought this body to my grandfather's house. My dad was five in those days, right? And they took the door off the hinges and took a chair, put it here and a chair there, and laid the door across the chairs to make a slab, and picked the body up and laid it on the door. Then they took all of the clothes off of my grandfather's cousin. A doctor came and plugged the bullet holes up with cotton where he'd been shot so he wouldn't bleed anymore. See you didn't have a mortuary, anything like that. And then they went over to the boarding house where he lived and got his suit. All the miners had one good suit in those days, I guess. If you can imagine a five-year-old watching this, they put the suit on him. And then they went to the carpenter shop at the company and got a pine box. That's who made the coffins in those days. They brought the pine box over. Then they took the body off the door and put it down in the coffin, nailed it shut right there in the living room, took him to the railroad station and shipped his body back to Kentucky where he was from. And then put the door back on its hinges. Dad told that story just like he saw it yesterday morning. He had the best memory, best storyteller you ever heard, and he never missed a beat telling that story. So, I heard lots and lots of stories about the Union and coal mining growing up.

Kin to the Blizzards

Kline: Somebody told me that you are somehow related to the Blizzards?

Roberts: Oh, yeah. Oh, yes.

Kline: I've always wondered about Ma Blizzard.

Roberts: Ma Blizzard raised my mother. I've tried to figure out exactly what age my mom started living with Ma Blizzard. She must have been around ten or eleven. And she lived with Ma Blizzard until she got married. When Dad and she got married, they didn't want to tell Ma Blizzard. How's that going to work? My mom told me the story that Dad was frightened to tell Ma. But they eventually did. My mother worked in Ma Blizzard's restaurant for years and years.

Kline: And that was where?

Roberts: Eskdale. Eskdale was a very significant place because when miners went on strike on Cabin Creek in 1912 and 1913, everything on Cabin Creek was owned by the coal company, except Eskdale. They used to joke and say that their town was the "Free State" of Eskdale. And Ma Blizzard gave the striking miners (evicted from the company houses) property to put their tents on. That's how she got the name of Mother Blizzard by the miners. They thought of her the same as they thought of Mother Jones. Mother Jones used to stay at Mother Blizzard's home. A lot of people didn't know that. My grandmother Harlow recalled that when she was a little girl, Mother Jones came to stay with Mother Blizzard. When she was older, she used to tell me about meeting Mother Jones at Mother Blizzard's. So my family, yeah, they were very proud the fact that they built the Union in West Virginia. They also, you know, historically knew that Mother Jones and others were very famous in the annals of labor history.

Bill Blizzard (who led the march on Blair Mountain in August of 1921) was Mother Blizzard's son. He would be my great-uncle. And he was my grandmother Harlow's brother. And I never really met him because at that time I was, you know, a teenager. Even before that his career was over and finished with the Union. But I heard a lot about him from people talking. My mother used to say a lot of the Union officials came into the restaurant on Cabin Creek, from District 17 and other places. So she got to meet a lot of those people in her lifetime. They called it Ma Blizzard's Restaurant. Oh, I remember that restaurant—.

Kline: Was there a counter to sit at or tables? What did she serve?

Roberts: Oh, hot dogs, hamburgers, and barbeques pretty much. And I guess they had pies and stuff like that. But she told me she served many a coal miner, many a Union official, sandwiches.

My mother told me this story. People could sell beer, you know. And Bill Blizzard thought that Ma Blizzard ought to get a beer license, start selling beer because there's lots of money to be made. Believe it or not, coal miners like to drink beer occasionally, not to mention everybody else on Cabin Creek. But Frank Blizzard—Frank Blizzard was Bill's brother—eventually took over Ma Blizzard's restaurant and turned it into a beer tavern. One end of it, ironically, sold ice cream and hot dogs. And they had curb service. The other end became pretty much a beer joint after Mother Blizzard gave it up. So Frank took it over and he sold beer for many, many years there. And they still sold sandwiches. But they had an ice cream–like custard stand attached to the other end, so people could pull in and get curb service or walk in and get ice cream, or go inside and drink beer. Lots and lots of folks came to the place. It was like "the place to go" on Cabin Creek in those days, I guess. But when Mother Blizzard had it, for the most part it was a restaurant.

Immigrants and Strikes on Cabin Creek
Roberts: In 1912, there were 6,000 people on strike on Cabin Creek. Mother Jones spoke at the Cabin Creek junction. They said

that there were 6,000 people in attendance. So, coal mining was very labor intensive in those days. And thousands and thousands of people were working in those coal mines.

Kline: And you probably heard about every kind of language spoken, didn't you?

Roberts: If you go back and read the history of the United Mine Workers, it was formed by immigrants when they had the first convention in Columbus, Ohio, in 1890, on January 25th. That is amazing that they were able to organize it because they really couldn't speak to each other. The [*United Mine Workers*] *Journal* used to be printed, I think, in twenty-some different languages. You know, I've heard people came from all over the world to mine coal in places like West Virginia and eastern Kentucky. So when they had the first convention, I guess they had to have somebody try to interpret for them. And the union they formed is still around. That's just an amazing story. I think the movie *Matewan* does a great job of depicting what it was like to be on strike with people from different countries and different cultures trying to understand each other and still stand up against the companies.

Shopping at Kroger

Roberts: Dad told another story about how he and Mom had the audacity one time to go to Kroger and shop. Kroger is a big food chain everyone in West Virginia is familiar with. Later he reports to work and the superintendent comes out and asks him if he's been shopping somewhere besides the company store. And Dad acknowledged that they had. And the superintendent said, "I want to tell you something, we have just as good products at our company stores as they do anywhere else and we expect our employees to shop at the company store." And that day they gave Daddy a bad place to load coal. In those days, you were hand-loading the coal. They would send you wherever they wanted you to load coal. Well, they sent him to work in a place that had water standing in it as a punishment for shopping at Kroger. So there were ways to force you to deal with the company store. We always did deal at the company store when I was growing up. We used to go to the Kayford Company Store, Acme Company Store, Leewood Company Store, Rhonda Company Store. When I started work in the mines, I bought my first pair of boots, my hard hat and belt at the Winifrede Company Store—it was owned by Carbon Fuel—because it was hard to find hard hats and a belt and boots anywhere else. So, the company stores were around when I started mining coal in the 1970s.

First Day in the Hole

Kline: Tell us, you must have some memories of your first day in the mines, do you?

Roberts: (Laughs) Yes. (Laughs) I think I was twenty-three. I'd been in the army, been to Vietnam. And then went to work in the mines. The first day was a Friday, I remember very well. Scared to death, terrified. Although my dad had been a miner all his life, I was nervous as I could be. Started on the day shift. And in those days someone had to sign a paper to be responsible for you. A miner named Joe Pratt, who was in his fifties, signed for me that day. I still remember it very well. The man-trip [a conveyance that transported workers to the coal face] was outside on the tracks. Didn't have a cover over it because the mine was too low for a canopy. The average height in that mine was forty-two inches but, it got down to as low as thirty-six inches in some places. And when you laid down on the top of the cars that made up the man-trip, you had to lay on your side. And if you raised up, you could touch the top of the coal seam as you rolled underground from the drift mouth. And Joe Pratt says to me, "Son, don't raise up.

If you raise up you'll get your head tore off." That was the first instruction he gave me. Said, "Don't raise up, you'll get your head tore off." So as we rode underground, I'm lying on my side and I can see the top right above me. I'm looking around this mine and I'm thinking, "Oh my goodness!" And the further we went underground, the more nervous I got.

We get to where our section is, and all these older guys jump off the man-trip and they just take off walking. But you can't stand up. I can't figure out how to walk. They were walking all bent over like this and just flying up the section. I'm hitting my head and I'm falling down. It was a chore just to get up on the section. And then they gave me a shovel and I shoveled all day, cleaning the ribs. You can't have loose coal in the ribs, right? You've got to clean that up and put it in the middle of the walkways so that the loading machine can pick it up. And I'm doing that and I'm thinking after a while, "It's got to be lunchtime," you know. "They've forgot about me," is just what I'm thinking, and then more time goes by. And then gosh, "It's got to be three o'clock. They forgot about me altogether here." And then after what I thought was three o'clock passed, they came to me and told me it was eleven o'clock. And it seemed like an eternity. They let me go eat. When I went back to work from eating, I was loading or shoveling coal again. By the time I got back outside, I was exhausted. And we didn't work on Saturdays in those days. Some people did. They posted notice of who they wanted to work. Saturday, I could hardly get out of bed. I was trying to walk, hurt from the top of my head to the tip of my toes. And then on Monday I had to go back and try it again. And I'm thinking, "I wonder if I can do this?" But I made myself to go back. After about a month of this, you finally get used to it. You learn how to walk, you learn how to get around in the mines. Things become more familiar to you, but it took a while. It was hard. But I stuck it out. I had a wife and two kids to take care of. So it was interesting to say the least. It was hard.

But after while, I think coal miners don't look at their jobs any different than someone going to work in an auto factory or, for that matter, going to work in a studio. I was on *Crossfire* one time on CNN. And one of the panelists said to me, "So people here"—he was talking about Washington—"can't understand why anybody wants to work in the mines." I said, "Well, people where I came from can't understand why anybody wants to live in Washington. So there you go." (Laughs) They said, "You've got a good point." But coal miners, once they got used to mining coal, that's the workplace. And after a while you don't think about it any differently than anybody else going to work might think about their workplace. We know we are working in a dangerous place. We know we have to look after our safety and look after each other. But it's not like we get up every day dreading to go to work or hating to go to work. It's our job, right? And we take a lot of pride in it.

A Favorite Photo: The Pittston Strike

Kline: When we came in, out in the hallway we saw a picture of you exchanging pleasantries with a—

Roberts: (Laughs)

Kline: State policeman? Tell us about that.

Roberts: That is one of my favorite pictures, perhaps ever. That was during the Pittston strike when we had taken over and occupied the Moss 3 preparation plant. We had ninety-nine of our members and one minister go into the preparation plant on a Sunday afternoon—caught them off guard. I say caught them off guard, that would have been the company, their security team, which was an advanced security team, and the state police. The state police, we determined, switched out [changed their shifts] about that time on Sundays. The ones finishing up their shift were leaving and others were arriving to work at about that time. So they weren't prepared. And we rushed in, took over the preparation plant. And then we had—

Cecil Roberts (with glasses) leads fellow strikers at Moss 3 Pittston mine in September 1989.

Kline: Ninety-nine?

Roberts: Ninety-nine strikers and one minister—but we had 1,200, 1,400 strikers outside—rushed in by car caravan about same moment. We held that plant from Sunday afternoon until Wednesday night. And no one could come in or go out without our permission. And the police, the U.S. marshals, judges, federal and state, none of them could do anything about it. They fined us very heavily, obviously. But that was a significant victory for the

Union, and it sent a loud clear message to the company that we were not going away. So about the second day there, the U.S. marshals came out to serve us an injunction ordering us out of there. The state police were gathered around also. So in that picture you see the state police, but there were also U.S. marshals there with guns on. And we're into a conversation with them about how they were going to serve all one hundred people that were in the plant, as well as ourselves and John Cox, who was with me, and others. By the time that ended on Wednesday—we always had rallies on Wednesday nights in St. Paul—since we were at the preparation plant, we just had a rally there. And the *Roanoke Times* ran a story and they estimated a crowd of about 5,000 outside that plant on Wednesday night. They said it was like "a Billy Graham crusade at altar call time" is how they described it. There was music and speeches. We had the miners from inside the plant come out and drop their backpacks and everything in a truck. And got them out of there while we had a big crowd on hand so the police could not identify them and arrest them. It was probably a highlight of my career during the Moss 3 takeover in the Pittston strike of September 1989.

The West Virginia State Museum

Kline: Well now, I'll tell you. I got my first look at the *Coal* exhibit at the State Museum at the Culture Center in Charleston last week. And I went there having seen your letter of July 26, in which you laid out some concerns you had about the exhibit. And having recently seen the exhibit I can't find that it reflects the details you've been telling me over the last forty minutes about your own life in the coalfields. The story just isn't there. It doesn't come alive. You would think the people who developed that exhibit, that none of them had ever seen a coal mine or even talked to a coal miner. None of this you're telling me is reflected in that exhibit. And I'm wondering how you feel about it.

Roberts: I think, as I looked at the museum, maybe I'm wrong, but it seemed to me that they were trying to speak to how they would like to see our history perceived, as opposed to how our history is. (Laughs) What I mean by that is, I think the State—and I understand their perspective on this—wanted to project to the rest of the country a better image of the coal industry in West Virginia. So they worked from that perspective, as opposed to working from a perspective of let's tell the actual, factual history of coal mining and the Union and the struggles and trials and tribulations that existed throughout the years.

Two things I think that jump out at you. First, the exhibit's assertion of how great the coal company stores were, that they were really the forerunners of the credit card. I mean, that is the most absurd description imaginable with respect to what the company stores were. You are really stretching things a mile to say that the company stores were the forerunners of credit cards and how wonderful that was. I don't think there are very many people who would say, "I wish the company stores would come back. I wish I can go back to that company store again and pay more [than other local stores charged]. I wish I was obligated to go back to the company store." You just never hear anyone say that.

Another [detail of the exhibit] that was totally misleading, I thought, and inappropriate, is the way they describe the Monongah explosion. That was the worst industrial accident in the history of our country, period. The official number of miners killed there is listed as 362, but the real number is probably closer to 500 people, because in those days, you could take someone with you, maybe your brother or your son, whatever—and they were contract miners [and not officially counted]—to go in and help you load coal. So the truth is, I don't think anyone knows the actual number killed. It is probably closer to 500 than 362. For whatever reason, some museum designer felt it necessary to say how wonderful Christmas was that year because the company gave the grieving families bonuses. There is no way that could have been a wonderful Christmas. What is the point of saying that? I mean, this is the greatest tragedy in our industrial history. But we think we have an obligation somehow to say that it was not a bad Christmas? It was a terrible Christmas! It would be a horrendous Christmas for everybody who lost a father or son or brother or friend. I thought it was just totally, completely self-serving, a real slap in the face to all those miners who died there and their families and friends. I mean, if you read the account that McAteer wrote about in his book, the most recent accounting of the tragedy there: in the weeks following the explosion at Monongah, three other major mine disasters occurred, prompting the last month of 1907 to be nicknamed "Black December." In the final tally, 3,241 American miners were killed on the job that year, the largest number killed in a single year in this country's history. In spite of such horrific accidents, many mining operations, including Monongah, continued to ignore recognized safety precautions, using open candles instead of shielded lamps, employing cheap dynamite instead of controllable explosives, and skipping tests that would detect methane gas. Such practices were already being followed in Europe.

Almost of all those miners were immigrants. And some of them hadn't brought their families to West Virginia or the United States yet. So it was even tough trying to figure out who to notify. It was just a horrendous and terrible time in West Virginia. I mean, why can't we just say that this was a terrible tragedy. It was painful and it was hurtful and leave it at that, because that's the truth. And for someone to say, "Let's think of something good say about the company here." (Laughs) Why? You don't have to do that. If something happened, say it and move on.

I'm proud of our industry now for trying to make mines safer, and I think 95 percent of the companies are trying to do what's right by improving safety. But you got 5 percent out there that the federal government and the state government just have to make do what's right. They just have to do that. That's why we have laws. It keeps good companies continuing to be good companies and bad companies, making them do what's right. And that's just the way it is. I don't think you take history and say, "Well, what can we say good about the other side here?" That's not really history, is it? When you have this tragedy, what's the point of talking about the bonuses that somebody got? Goodness gracious. It was not certainly a good Christmas, right?

Kline: It couldn't have been.

Roberts: Yeah.

Kline: So what do you think that the museum's going to do, or what would you like to see the museum do about all of this?

Roberts: To me a museum tells me a story and it tells the truth. Whatever the truth is, that's what they should tell. I don't think there's very many people who would say, "I wish the company stores would come back. I wish I owed my soul to the company store." Who can you hear saying that? No one. If the company stores were that great they'd still be here, wouldn't they? They are not here anymore and there is a reason for that: because they weren't a good thing. They might have been a necessary thing in some instances. But it doesn't mean that they were good thing. Let's just tell the truth about company stores, right? Let's tell the truth about the tragedies we've had and just leave it at that.

Sugarcoating the Truth
Roberts: Someone when they put this museum together said, "We have an obligation here to figure out something good to say about both sides." I don't really know, in the case of museums, if

you have sides. It's just a history of your state, right? You don't have an obligation to say something good about the coal companies if you say something bad about the coal companies. We should be proud of the industry we have now just trying to do better and provide jobs. That doesn't mean that a hundred years ago it was like that, or fifty years ago it was like that. The truth is we had to bring the government kicking and screaming to the aid of the coal miners. The government didn't come and drag the coal miners kicking and screaming to have better laws. The coal miners had to give up theirs lives, had to strike and fight and everything else to get the government to be on their side. That's the truth. That is as true as it can be. And you can't sugarcoat that. You can't change that. That's a fact. Museums are supposed to be about facts and history and what happened, not what you would've liked to have happen, see happen, not what you wish had happened. But is that exhibit telling the truth when 100 other people are saying, "That is not way it was?" So I think museums are historical presentations that should be factual.

Kline: And do you feel that that should be their obligation?

Roberts: I don't think there is any doubt that it should be their obligation. If you're going to have a museum—. If it is not a museum that's presenting facts, call it something else. "This is the way we wish it was." (Laughs) How about that? (Laughs) I don't know what you call that. It's some kind of presentation, but it's not a factual one.

Kline: Do you hold out any hope that they are going to straighten that up?

Roberts: I always hold out hope for everything, but it doesn't mean that it's going to happen. I don't know why this museum was put together in the manner that it was. They claimed that they had all these historians that verified what they placed in the museum. I would like to have an opportunity to meet these historians, and maybe sit around a table like this and let's talk about it.

Kline: With these historians?

Roberts: Yes, whoever they are. Where did they get—? What books, what kinds of authority did they have? I mean, are they experts in this field? Are they really historians? Where did they get their information? What did they rely on to come to these kinds of conclusions? Who did they talk to? Out of hundreds and thousands of, perhaps a million people who lived through this, what percentage of those people did they talk to who gave them this kind of description of the way life was in those days, which is obviously [in the case of the *Coal* exhibit at the Cultural Center] very contrary to what most of people remember?

I think it's really important for tourists to see [authentic exhibits] and come away saying good things about West Virginia. There are a lot of good things to say about West Virginia. But you can't make the Civil War sound like something nice, can you? You can't take the civil rights movement and sugarcoat it and say it was all just peachy keen and fine and dandy. Bull Connor was Bull Connor, right? You can work all day long and you can't make him a good person. And you can't make people who murdered civil rights leaders good people, can you? You can't make company stores good things either. It might have been convenient, it might have been necessary in a lot of instances, but you can't say these were wonderful things for coal miners. It just wasn't that way. Many miners were head-over-heels in debt to them. And the truth is that if the miners had had more flexibility, more freedom to shop, they could have gotten by more economically than they did shopping at the company stories. But even that is not the thing that really stands out to me. It's the characterization of the Monongah disaster and trying to make Christmas seem like a good time or applaud companies if they did give money to families. I'm sure they did, but that doesn't make this thing go away or make it any better.

> "A history museum is as good as the history that goes into it, and the West Virginia State Museum is based on the very best scholarship available to this generation. Top historians were involved from start to finish and their thoughtful work underlies every part of our spectacular new museum."
>
> —*Ken Sullivan,*
> *West Virginia Humanities Council*

State Museum Historians

Dr. Ron Eller	Dr. Jerry Thomas	Dr. Ron Lewis
Dr. John Williams		Dr. Ken Sullivan

> "The historians were not paid for their work, so it didn't make a lot of sense to keep revising the text and asking them to review the material a second time (for free)."
>
> —*Stan Bumgardner, creative director for the*
> *West Virginia State Museum, March 9, 2010*

Ardent Socialist?

Kline: What about referring to Bill Blizzard and other leaders of the march in 1921 as ardent socialists?

Roberts: (Laughs) First of all, how did they know what Bill Blizzard's views were? I think, I've actually heard that Bill Blizzard might have been a Republican. (Laughs) I don't know if that's the same as a socialist or not. It might be. (Laughs) I don't know what Bill Blizzard's politics were. But let's be fair here. Anyone that's ever stood up for workers in the history of this country has been called something, and "a socialist" is one of the things that people might lay on you, or worse, if you are fighting for folks. Some people believe that you should just support the capitalistic system and the people in power. That's why 1% of our country is doing fine. And 99% of us aren't. If 99% of us would like to see things better, what does that make us? The 1% thinks we're socialists, right?

Kline: I'm sure.

Roberts: I'm sure they do. And I'm sure they call us names from time to time. But I think we are just trying to get our fair share of what the capitalistic system produces. And I don't think it is fair to call Bill Blizzard anything in particular. But you have to look at the times too. I think Frank Keeney openly acknowledged that he was a socialist, but back in those days it wasn't that uncommon, right? I mean he was standing up for workers. Eugene Debs ran for the presidency several times and got millions of votes, right?

What they are trying to do [in the *Coal* exhibit] is to use today's definition of what someone might perceive of as a "socialist" or left-leaning person and apply it to make this [historic figure] seem like a radical and out of touch. But in those days, both Keeney and Bill Blizzard were very popular people, regardless of their politics.

Kline: Well, the exhibit nowhere refers to the coal operators as "rabid capitalists," either.

Roberts: You might have applied something even worse than that to them.

Kline: Sure.

Roberts: But there is no historical benefit in name-calling either to coal operators or, for that matter, to leaders of the Union. I think what we should do is to state facts about how workers were exploited. I don't recall reading anywhere in that museum that workers were exploited. Now, does that make it untrue? It's absolutely true that workers were exploited. Workers who were being paid by the ton back in 1912 and 1913 and all through the 1920s had a company checkweighman (to tally the car load), and you had to load 2,500 or 3,000 pounds to get credit for a "company ton." The company checkweighman lied about how much you mined. On payday days, if you don't get any money, what are you? But by the time they deducted for the company store, the company house, and the company doctor, and the company tools you used, you got zero. You worked sixteen hours a day loading coal and if you didn't get paid, what does it make you? It makes you what? A slave! I'm reminded that as late as 1985, Don Blankenship made a speech in Huntington and he said, "If everyone would work for nothing, everyone would have a job." That is absolutely true. But that makes you what? A slave, which is the same thing that you had in 1912, 1913, up through the 1920s.

Weekends and Vacations

Roberts: This situation existed until the Wagner Act was passed in the mid-'30s giving people legal right to join the Union. What happened when they had the legal right? Why did hundreds, millions of people, for that matter, rush to join unions when the Wagner Act passed? Because they wanted to have a better way of life. And when did the middle class come of age? It was when workers had the right to join unions. And then they could get paid a fair day's pay for a fair day's work. They could have vacations, and they could have pensions. They could have health care. They could actually send their kids off to school.

And people today badmouth the unions like they were the worst thing in the world. A lot of those people ought to go back and look at how they got those benefits: because some unions or a group of unions fought for those things. Until we had the legal right in this country to join unions, we had none of those things. That's when things got better in the coalfields. That's when things got better in the auto industry, steel industry. That's when things got better across this country and the middle class was born. So, I always say when you see a union person, thank them for the vacation you are going on, or the health care and wages you have, or personal leave days, floating vacation days, or whatever you have.

Kline: Like the weekend?

Roberts: Weekends, yeah, brought you by organized labor, right? (Laughs)

Kline: Wow. This has been great.

Roberts: Oh, good.

Kline: Is there anything else that you'd like to talk about, or that I should ask you?

Roberts: I just think we owe so much to those people who went before us. Up until the passage of the Wagner Act, working-class people were not in the middle class. Coal miners were still strug-gling. When the Wagner Act was passed, millions of people joined unions. And people went on marches and sit-down strikes in the auto industry, and strikes in the coal industry. Then we had Lewis who fought for the 1946–47 Health and Retirement [Funds], health and retirement provisions of the contract and brought us all into the middle class, starting in 1935 and moving up into the '50s. And for many years in this country, if you contributed to the production of the auto industry, or contributed to the production of coal, you got your fair share of what had been produced. As you look around now, the top 1% is getting the most of it. And there is not much left for the rest of us. That's what's wrong with the country now. We need, I think, more power in organized labor to give the people a stronger, more powerful voice in order to get a greater share of the wealth they are producing so that all of us can enjoy the benefits of middle-class [living], not just that a tiny fraction of our society.

THE SOUND OF SILENCE

During the tourist season of 2016, I took a tour of the Beckley Exhibition Coal Mine and Youth Museum in Beckley, West Virginia. The facility is owned by the City of Beckley. After approximately thirty minutes under-ground the following exchange took place:

Wess: Why wasn't the Union mentioned in the tour . . . as far as the men getting together and saying we don't want that unsafe stuff, we don't want the scrip?

Guide: Well . . . there wasn't no union until the '30s. . . . Now I know quite a bit about it. . . . I know the Union was formed in 1906. Three companies came together in Columbus and formed the United Mine Workers . . . but . . . we don't say too much about it . . . we don't say too much about the company stores . . . you know . . . [whispering] I don't want to end up in trouble.

The United Mine Workers was formed in 1890 and not by three companies! —ed.

Kline: You have spoken now twice about being introverted as a younger man—.

Roberts: (Laughs) Yeah.

Kline: I wonder if you can remember the moment when you—? Or was there a particular situation when you found your voice?

Roberts: I think it started in the army, and then, I think, continued on and probably developed to a great extent when I became a local Union officer and spokesperson for that small group of people I was representing. Ours was a pretty radical local, and you had to learn to speak up for what you believed and defend yourself in arguments. And then I was given an opportunity to come out of the mines for a couple of weeks. I received training from the Federal Mediation and Conciliation Service and was given an opportunity to teach classes for four months. That's where I think things really took off for me, to stand in front of other miners day in and day out, teaching classes on labor history, how to file grievances, past practices and customs, all these things that help people become better local Union representatives. The Union had me doing that for four months back in 1976. And that's probably what opened every door to me for moving up in the Union, which I think really blossomed into where I am now.

Kline: So, is your experience a reflection of the mission in the United Mine Workers to provide rank-and-file education?

Roberts: Yes, this was something Arnold Miller envisioned in District 17, being his home district, and actually paid for this. I think Arnold had a lot of great ideas, quite frankly. And I think his health probably prevented him from reaching the pinnacle he would like to have achieved. Arnold actually envisioned having a continuing education department at the UMWA to educate miners and particularly leaders, an ongoing, never-ending educational process growing out of an educational department at the Union. And if we could do that now, it would be something great. We do a lot of education but we don't have what I would call an educational department here. Miller had that vision, and I think it is a correct one, all the way back in the '70s. We still do education for our safety committee men because we have a heavy emphasis here on protecting workers. But the earlier plan in the '70s would have expanded from that, to teach labor history and contract education, how to present cases and win cases, what you need to be good witnesses, things of that nature. I loved the labor history part of it, myself. That's when I started trying to learn as much as I could about our history so that I could teach it to others. Arnold Miller had a lot of great ideas. Unfortunately his health didn't allow him to act on all of them.

Kline: Thank you very much.

Roberts: Thank you. I enjoyed it.

Hidden Coffins Unearth Needed History

Fr. John S. Rausch

Fr. John Rausch, a Glenmary priest, has served as director of the Catholic Committee on Appalachia and was the recipient of the 2007 Teacher of Peace Award, presented by Pax Christi USA.

AT THE INTERSECTION OF RT. 612 AND SCARBRO ROAD, JUST outside Oak Hill, West Virginia, the Whipple Colliery Company Store stands as a two-story structure with a massive flight of steps that leads a visitor into the central merchandising room of the store's commissary. Just off from the spacious room a hand-operated freight elevator connects the basement storage area of this late nineteenth-century building with the main floor and the top floor frequently festooned for the owner's ballroom dances.

Curiously, a secret space is sandwiched between these first and second floors. This hidden area, just five feet high and accessible only by elevator, housed the coffins the company deemed necessary as a cost of digging coal. Keeping the coffins out of sight reduced the stress on both wives and miners who shopped at the store, but they played an integral role in coal mining and were needed almost every day.

"The coffins would service three mines in the area," says Joy Lynn, co-owner and curator of the Whipple Company Store Museum and Learning Center. "Some days they'd need forty, some days they'd need ten, some days one, and some days sixty. We're talking about the period between 1893 and 1930."

Learning History, Seeing a Vision

Unfortunately, today few Americans grasp the significance of the sufferings our forebearers endured to create the working conditions that insure a more dignified workplace. Child labor laws, the eight-hour workday, workman's compensation, Social Security and retirement programs, health and safety laws—all taken for granted today—represent progressive reforms supported by organized labor, the Church, and people of faith.

The point: people of faith especially need to learn where the coffins of history are kept! Unlike the Ten Commandments that were given by God and inscribed in the heart of every believer, the social teachings of the Catholic Church came from reflections about earning a living in a capitalist system. For more than a century the Church observed the conditions of workers, the abuse of immigrants, and the power of capital to manipulate creation and communities. From those observations it established social principles for engaging in commercial life while treating workers with fairness and justice. While not strictly based on class analysis, these theological reflections proclaim a fundamental option for the poor and strive to balance the rights of individuals with their call to community. Not as a rugged individual or as someone lost in an amorphous collective, the Church sees each worker as a person-in-community who shares dignity and vision with coworkers who are brothers and sisters.

As globalization, new technologies, and a greater awareness of environmental concerns change the nature of work, the Church's social principles continue to challenge individual workers and structures to ask what the economic system is doing for people, what is it doing to people, and how people are participating. Without a sense of history and an awareness of the present, no realistic vision will inspire the future. And, without a vision, the people will perish. In a sense, people of faith today wonder where the coffins are kept.

Early Working Conditions

With the flowering of the Industrial Revolution in the latter part of the nineteenth century the demand for coal grew exponentially to fuel the steel mills and electrical generating plants dotting the countryside. Frequently, safety concerns took a backseat to the demands for production.

In 1869, the Avondale Colliery located in Luzerne County, Pennsylvania, suffered the largest human loss to that date with 110 miners killed when the wooden breaker constructed over the only exit shaft caught fire, trapping and suffocating the workers below. That era saw miners die daily from rock falls, premature blasts, or railway car accidents.

The deadliest year for American mining, 1907, witnessed the deaths of 3,242 workers with hundreds at a time losing their lives. Monongah, West Virginia, became the worst mining disaster in U.S. history when a blast caused by the ignition of methane gas and coal dust killed 362 workers officially, but because family members—frequently sons and even wives—customarily dug coal with the miners to make their minimal wage, historians think the number could have exceeded 500 fatalities. Just two weeks later at Darr, Pennsylvania, another 239 workers, mainly Hungarian immigrants, perished from a similar cause. During this era mining companies proved callous and cavalier about human safety, striving instead to protect the expensive mine mules and ponies at the expense of their cheap and abundant immigrant labor force. The twentieth century alone saw over 100,000 coal miners killed in U.S. mines with an untold larger number suffocating from black lung, or "miner's asthma."

Working conditions in most industries put profits before people and set workers, with few rights, against bosses with little mercy. The storied Triangle Shirtwaist Factory fire, as one of America's worst industrial accidents, demonstrates the disregard for workers. In 1911, on a Saturday afternoon when workers began thinking about their Sunday off, a fire started on the eighth floor of the ten-story Asch Building in Manhattan where the Triangle Company occupied the top three floors with 500 workers. The flames spread quickly to the upper floors trapping many amid the burning fabric and trimmings that lay bundled and loose in numerous piles. Witnesses reported the horror of seeing workers, many embracing one another, leap to their deaths from windows as the fire engulfed them. The tragic toll numbered 146 dead, mostly immigrant girls and women, with scores more seriously injured, because the two freight elevators failed as an escape after the owners locked the stairwell doors.

More than a century ago workers regularly logged twelve-hour shifts six days a week. In 1880, one sixth of American workers (1,118,000) were children under the age of sixteen. In 1889 alone, 22,000 railroad workers were killed or injured on the job. Because wages fluctuated with the economy, the Carnegie Steel Company, in 1892, cut pay between 18 percent and 26 percent, leading to the Homestead Strike that ended in bloody violence. A little more than a century ago the human dignity of American workers was sacrificed to a new wave of industrialization.

The Dignity and Rights of Workers

This history represented the type of conditions that prompted people of faith to speak out about human dignity and the rights of workers. Pope Leo XIII wrote his groundbreaking encyclical *Rerum Novarum* in 1891, which rejected both an unbridled capitalism that could deny workers their God-given human dignity and an ultra-powerful state that could destroy their self-determined human initiative. In that seminal document the Catholic Church clearly promoted unions, a just wage, and the renewal of the social order.

For people of faith, however, the dignity of workers rests not on any privilege afforded by the state, or any argument offered from economic theory, but on moral and ethical laws that originate from the nature of the human person. Each worker is made in the image and likeness of God and we are all our brother's (and sister's) keeper. This theological statement forms the basis for the dignity of each worker and the worker's call to community and the common good.

To protect their dignity and to recognize all people as social beings, workers have a right to form a union. Because the employer has so much power, unions act as a countervailing force to level the playing field so workers can demand safe and decent working conditions. They also need a just wage to maintain their families, health care to insure their strength, and retirement benefits to guarantee a dignified old age. Because workers are not machines, they need periods of rest, not only to rejuvenate their bodies for more work, but to become fully integrated persons, i.e. people who can appreciate beauty and the arts, and grow spiritually.

With this view of human dignity, the notion of work becomes something beyond simply earning a livelihood. Work participates in divine activity. God worked. God rested on the seventh day after God worked to create the heavens and the earth. Then God invited humanity into the labor force by placing humanity (Adam) in the garden "to care and cultivate it" (Gen. 2:15). So humanity becomes a co-gardener with God! Yes, people work to earn a livelihood, but they also work for self-fulfillment, to feel good about themselves, and ultimately to contribute to society and make a difference.

A celebrated parable describes a reporter interviewing three workers at a building site. Asked what he was doing, the first responded, "I'm laying bricks." The second ventured a further description: "I'm building a wall." But the third worker shared his experience with enthusiasm and glee: "Can't you see, I'm building a cathedral!" Same activity, same work, different vision.

Begin with Solidarity

Workers need a way to build "their cathedrals" at work, and unions offer the best structure for workers' rights. Yet one myth with wide currency says that unions, once needed in the past to counter unregulated capitalism, are now passé because of today's environmental and labor laws.

In July 2002, nine coal miners working the Quecreek Mine near Somerset, Pennsylvania, punched through a wall to an abandoned mine and felt the fury of 150 million gallons of water gushing through the breach. Scrambling for their lives the miners ran in crouched position through a four-and-a-half-foot-high passage seeking higher ground as the rising water engulfed them. With the water to their necks, then their chins, the men pulled themselves along the main conveyor belt and finally found an eighteen-foot by thirty-foot patch of high ground where they rested and waited for help.

On the Pennsylvania hillside the drama took place on two stages—above with the rescue workers and below among the trapped miners. Topside, the rescue team used global satellite positioning equipment—with a dash of common sense—to target the air pocket. The most advanced technology and the sharpest engineering minds worked to free the miners.

Below, the men lived "nine for nine"—everyone would survive, or the team would die together. Drenched from fighting the water, they sat back-to-back to preserve body heat. Two men sandwiched a third shaking from hypothermia. They encouraged one another and kept their spirits high. Through their belts they looped plastic coated cable and tied themselves together.

Finally, after seventy-eight hours, cheers erupted when the men emerged one by one from the escape cage to the glare of cameras and the embrace of rescuers.

On balance, technology contributed its part to the rescue, but the miners' spirit proved essential. Tethered to one another "nine for nine," the miners offered the world an important metaphor by demonstrating their code of solidarity.

Yet at a hearing about the Quecreek accident some months later, Jeffrey Mihallik, a safety committeeman from the United Mine Workers of America, said the accident should never have happened and reminded the panel that under any UMWA contract union members can refuse to work in unsafe conditions. Nonunion miners, like those at Quecreek, do not enjoy such protection. They either go in or go home.

Discover the New Vision

Unions continue to play their traditional role safeguarding the rights of workers with contracts and political representation. Local union safety committees make union mines safer than nonunion mines by creating a "safety effect," thus lowering the serious injury and fatality rate. And unions not only secure higher wages for their own members but through the "threat effect" force nonunion mines to pay comparable wages to keep the union out. Also, the social milestones like child labor laws, Social Security, and the eight-hour day have fingerprints from the union movement all over them.

Yet today unions, with churches and progressive institutions, face the challenge of revising the self-image of workers and the middle class from rugged individualists to people of community. At the turn of the twentieth century industrial barons endeavored to split the working class by convincing people their self-interest lay in becoming consumers, thus weakening their allegiance to progressive groups. The emphasis began the long gradual shift to concern for individual gain without regard for the environment, the local community, or the common good.

Social commentator Msgr. George Higgins (1916–2002), known as the "labor priest," wrote: "American workers need a raise, but they need more than a raise. They need a vision—a vision of economic citizenship."

That economic citizenship means involvement in life beyond shopping. It entails a voice in the workplace, volunteering in the local community, and speaking out for a healthy environment. While social legislation wove a safety net intended for all, the fact remains that legislation gave it, and legislation can take it away. Without due vigilance the strands of labor's safety net can fray, or be cut, for short-term profits and the company's stock value.

Economic citizenship means shopping with regard for the dignity of the worker overseas and buying in solidarity with the worker in the local community. The "cheapest price" consideration must be balanced with the "social implication" of the purchase. And, with only one planet to sustain life, economic citizenship means practicing a stewardship of creation.

The Journey

How many strikes and marches, how many speeches and sermons, how many pieces of legislation it took during the history of labor to secure the minimal rights of workers! Labor historians can appreciate Avondale, Monongah, and Darr contributing to the vision that workers deserve a safe environment and a place of respect and dignity. People of faith can deepen that conviction with moral and ethical principles, but they must first reflect on where the coffins are hidden. The journey to a caring community where workers have a just wage with safe and dignified working conditions recalls the early labor vision that "an injury to one is an injury to all," which to people of faith sounds strangely similar to "Do unto others as you would have them do unto you."

When Miners March—A Review

Theresa Burriss, PhD

Theresa Burriss is director of Appalachian studies at Radford University. This review was first published in Appalachian Heritage.

William C. Blizzard. *When Miners March*. Edited by Wess Harris. Oakland, CA: PM Press, 2010. 408 pages with photos and appendices. Trade paperback, $21.95.

The recording and telling of history have proven to be troublesome for the critically minded as inconsistencies, innocent mistakes, and downright lies plague much of what readers are given as purported fact. Of course, as many realize, the "winners," or those in power, have traditionally written history and delivered it in a neat, seemingly indisputable package. Fortunately, honest historians do exist and attempt to convey more accurate pictures of historical events, often working from a grassroots or "in the trenches" perspective that provides room for the typically forgotten or intentionally overlooked players.

William C. Blizzard offers readers just such a retelling of history that gets at the truth of the labor struggles leading up to the 1921 Battle of Blair Mountain in West Virginia. His work, *When Miners March*, first titled *Struggle and Lose . . . Struggle and Win!*, is well-researched and documented, offering court transcripts, newspaper articles, letters, and written testimony from key players in the coal miners' efforts to unionize West Virginia.

The acquisition of the primary documents is due to William C. Blizzard's familial association with the labor fight, namely his father Bill Blizzard's role as a union organizer beginning as early as the Paint Creek and Cabin Creek skirmishes in 1912–13.

Offering a comprehensive history of coal in West Virginia, Blizzard starts his work in 1817 with the discovery of coal in the Kanawha Valley and then methodically moves forward, documenting the trials and tribulations of the miners in a year-by-year timeline. He even offers an historical interlude with primary accounts of the Ludlow, Colorado, massacre, where women and children, in addition to miners, were killed indiscriminately.

With Blizzard's meticulous attention to detail, readers come to appreciate the decades-long oppression exerted by the coal companies and understand how many local law enforcement agencies did the dirty bidding of those companies because they were paid handsomely to do so. Sheriff Don Chafin of Logan County is the most cited due to his ongoing ruthless oppression and oftentimes outright murder of miners and their families.

Even West Virginia's governors were not above bribery and openly worked to suppress the miners through policy and legislation, both at the state and federal levels, more often than not resorting to lies about the miners and their tactics to justify such suppression.

In the telling Blizzard also disputes many formerly accepted "truths" about the labor movement. For example, several other historians have placed C. Frank Keeney, UMWA District 17 President, and Fred Mooney, District 17 Secretary-Treasurer, in the middle of the Battle of Blair Mountain, leading the charge instead of Bill Blizzard, Sr. As son William Blizzard documents, however, the two union leaders were far removed from the site because of fears that they would fall to the same fate as Sid Hatfield and Ed Chambers, who'd been murdered in broad daylight by Baldwin-Felts "detectives," or gun thugs, on the steps of the McDowell County Courthouse. No one was ever brought to trial over these murders. William Petry, a UMWA organizer, explains, "Keeney and Mooney disappeared. Where they are I don't know, but I'm assured they are safe from the hired gunmen at present" (p. 308).

I must say that it helps to have a general understanding of the history of coal and labor in Appalachia before diving into this work. In fact, when teaching this work in college classes, I found my students responded to it much better after they read Denise Giardina's historical fiction on the subject, *Storming Heaven*, and Diane Gilliam's poetry companion, *Kettle Bottom*. The novel and poetry provided an entrée into the grittier details of *When Miners March*. My students noted that it's easy to get lost in the dates and lose track of the names without having a previous understanding, and even so, they needed to process everything in class to fully grasp the import of Blizzard's work. The history made a lasting impression on my students, however, when they visited many of the sites where the miners fought, set up tent colonies, and were buried. This experiential field trip offered a holistic education for my students, and I highly recommend it to fellow educators. Indeed, Blizzard's work came to life as the students made connections between all those historical details and the tangible evidence before them.

For the scholar and labor historian, *When Miners March* provides incredible insight into one of the most tumultuous times in our nation's labor history. For anyone who participates in any kind of labor force, the work illustrates how much we owe to the coal miners of Appalachia who lived, and oftentimes died, to secure basic freedoms and rights for all workers in the United States.

Written in Blood
The Impact of Widows and Orphans on the Passage of Kentucky Coal Mine Safety Legislation

Attorney Tony Oppegard as told to Michael Kline

What follows is based on a much longer interview recorded in Whitesburg, Kentucky on June 29, 2016, at the Appalachian Citizens' Law Center by Michael Kline, when Oppegard kicked back and recalled his thirty years of law practice in pursuit of miners' occupational health and safety in the coalfields of eastern Kentucky. Also present were law student interns Kara Good and Erica Cherry.

LET'S START BY TALKING ABOUT COAL MINES. IT'S SUCH A DANgerous occupation, where the slightest error could cause a miner loss of a limb, or cost him his life. In eastern Kentucky where I've done most of my cases, your average coal seam is forty to forty-eight inches high. That's your workplace. For the students who are here with us today, try to imagine that this table is your workplace. You're underneath this table for eight hours. You can't stand up, you're on your knees. If you're operating a piece of equipment, you're on your side. You can never stand up.

When you walk in the mine, you're what they call "duck walking," which means you're bent over and your back's right against the roof. And you're trying to get around as best you can, or you may have to crawl. And then you add the fact that it's dark underground. You may be working two, or three, or four—or seven miles under the mountain. There's nothing between you and the surface, other than a mountain over top of you and you're in a four-foot space crawling. It's dark. You've got your cap light, maybe the only light, except there's light on the equipment.

So if you're operating a piece of equipment at the face it will have headlights. You have this mammoth equipment underground. A continuous miner is thirty-seven feet long and nearly twenty feet wide. Roof-bolting machines are big pieces of equipment, and maneuvering them in these small spaces is challenging, so there's pinch points where people can be caught. You have electricity underground, so you have electricians. And electrocution is a common problem.

And you have methane, which is an explosive danger: any time you cut coal, methane is released, liberated. It's a natural part of the mining process. Even though every mine has methane the federal Mine Safety and Health Administration (MSHA) designates mines as "gassy" and "non-gassy." If you work below the water table you're going to have a gassy mine. And you have to be even more careful ventilating the mine, keeping fresh air in the mine to dilute the methane and to dilute the coal dust. Mines that are considered "non-gassy" still will have gas. It's just that they don't liberate as much gas as a gassy mine does.

Then you have coal dust, which is explosive, more explosive and powerful than methane. Coal dust can do two things: number one, it can destroy your lungs when you breathe it. That's what's called "respirable coal dust," very tiny particles that you don't see. But you must keep your ventilation up underground; you have to have fresh air pumped into the mine. Then when you get up to the face where the coal's being mined, you start using plastic curtains, ventilation curtains to direct the airflow. You direct it across the face. Let's say you have six entries, you're mining coal in these different places called "entries" or "headings," and you have to direct the fresh air into each heading where coal is being mined. Because when miners are cutting the coal, they're producing a tremendous amount of coal dust. It's suspended in the air. And federal law requires a certain velocity and quantity of air as you go into each place, to dilute that coal dust.

And then as you go across the face with the airflow, you're picking up gas, you're picking up dust contaminants. And then when you get to the end of the face, you have what's called the return air course. It goes out of the mine taking with it all the contaminants in the air. So you have the intake, which is fresh air, and the return, which is dirty air. And at the face you have a combination of the two with the air coming across to pick up the contaminants and sweep them out of the mine. So you have all these hazards.

And when miners breathe respirable coal dust, it gets into their lungs. You know, black lung has been an occupational hazard ever since coal mining began. And unfortunately in America we've not done a good enough job of preventing it, eliminating it. Coal dust has been greatly reduced in European countries where they basically don't have much black lung. But here, when the 1977 Act was passed they imposed standards for black lung. Permissible exposure limits, or what scientists call the PEL, is two milligrams per cubic meter—2 mg/m^3—of air underground. So just call it "the two milligram standard." Miners aren't supposed to be breathing any more than two milligrams of dust.

The theory was that if mines kept their dust below two milligrams per cubic meter, then miners could work a whole career underground, retire, and not have black lung—be able to breathe okay. But that just hasn't worked out, and there's still, I think, a thousand miners dying every year of black lung. Now a lot of these are retired miners, but it's an insidious disease that never gets better. Once you have black lung, it cannot be reversed; it just gets progressively worse. It's a horrible way to live and to die, because in the end miners finally choke to death. No longer able to work, they can hardly get around. They can't walk across the room without having shortness of breath.

A lot of miners end up on oxygen, and coal companies fight like hell to deny them their black lung disease benefits, which are very modest monthly payments. It's been an ongoing battle for years, sometimes decades, even thirty years, to resolve some of these cases. So miners have to worry about black lung disease underground, and that's one reason why you have to keep your ventilation curtains up, you have to have fresh air to sweep out this coal dust. But also, it's an explosion hazard, more explosive and powerful than methane.

And we've had a number of disasters over the years resulting in too many fatalities, like the South Mountain disaster near Norton, Virginia, on December 7, 1992. The South Mountain Coal Company it was. And I represented some of the widows in that case, investigating the disaster to see if there was a potential lawsuit and also representing them in front of a governor's commission in Virginia to make changes to the Mine Health and Safety Law.

At South Mountain a methane explosion turned into a coal dust explosion because there was so much coal dust suspended in the air and on the ribs and roof of the mine. Coal companies are supposed to take what's called rock dust—it's pulverized limestone, heavier than coal dust—and you can spread it by hand. In the old days a guy would walk around with a bag of pulverized limestone throwing handfuls of it on the walls of the mine, or what they called "the rib," on the roof, and on the floor to suppress the coal dust. Today they have these big machines with blowers, you know, they can drive through and blow it. If you go in a coal mine and it's well rock dusted, it should look completely white.

If you don't adequately rock dust—and that, for example, was the problem at Upper Big Branch—Upper Big Branch was initially a methane explosion with a secondary dust explosion. And if the mine isn't dusted for a distance, say, of two miles, then you have the potential for a fireball that's going to travel those two miles, picking up speed and more fuel as it goes, more coal dust as fuel, and killing and destroying everything in its path.

So for instance there was a disaster in Knott County, Kentucky. December 7, 1981, the Topmost Mine disaster, also called the Adkins disaster, because it was the Adkins Coal Company. Eight miners were killed, and it was a coal dust explosion not a methane explosion. In that mine they were shooting the coal. There are very few mines left today where they shoot coal—use explosives to dislodge the coal. Coal miners would go underground to the solid coal face where they would drill holes into the coal face with an electric drill. They would put explosives into the hole, tamp them in and use a clay "dummy" to keep the explosives in the hole. When you detonate it, the explosion stays in the hole.

Well here at Topmost, the Adkins disaster, the mine operator was, so sorry, too cheap to buy clay dummies at the price of twelve cents apiece. So without available clay stemming dummies to put in the holes on top of the explosives, the miners substituted little bags of rock dust, which weren't of sufficient weight and mass to contain the explosion. When the miners put off the shot, that is, detonated the explosives, the ignition burst back out into the atmosphere and ignited the coal dust. And once it ignited the coal dust, because the mine had not been sufficiently rock dusted, the explosion ripped through the mine. We heard testimony that at the drift mouth of the mine, the opening on the surface, that a fireball came all the way back and blew out of the entry way at the surface like a shotgun blast coming out of the coal mine, and eight guys were killed. There was one survivor walking near the drift mouth who was blown I don't know how many feet in the air and somehow survived.

I was a young attorney at the time working for Appalred Legal Services in Hazard, Kentucky, and I actually knew one of the widows who was a young woman almost nine months pregnant at the time her husband was killed. His name was James Slone and she was Beulah Slone. She grew up in nearby Pippa Passes in Knott County, where Alice Lloyd College is. And the mine was in a little community called Topmost. Her baby was born two weeks after the explosion, and that was their first child. So her daughter, who was named Jamie after her dad, never met him and has grown up without a father.

And six weeks later there was another coal dust explosion in neighboring Floyd County very similar to the disaster at Topmost. That's the RFH Mine. There were seven miners killed there. It happened on Mud Creek, right next to Eula Hall's legendary health clinic in Craynor. And so in a period of about six weeks you had two mine disasters in eastern Kentucky that killed fifteen miners. And in between, you had the Grundy, Tennessee, explosion where thirteen miners died. That's a total of twenty-eight miners killed in a period of about six weeks.

So I began representing all but one of the Topmost widows in the summer of 1982. On weekends we would go to shopping centers in eastern Kentucky with a petition that said, "The families of the Topmost disaster victims are asking MSHA to convene a public hearing." And we garnered almost 11,000 signatures over a two-month period. The widows went into their churches, went to shopping malls, et cetera, and we got all these thousands of people to sign.

We already knew *what* had happened at the mine, namely that it was a coal dust explosion, that the mine wasn't properly rock dusted, and we knew that the coal dust was ignited—again—because of the failure to use clay stemming dummies. But these were not the issues we were pursuing. We wanted to know *why* conditions were allowed to deteriorate to the point that they had. We wanted to know why it had happened, not technically how, but *why*. And those are the kinds of questions that you could explore at a public meeting.

The iconic Whitesburg newspaper, the *Mountain Eagle,* was a great crusader for mine safety in Appalachia. The editors, Tom and Pat Gish, opposed strip-mining, championed honest government, and examined all of the major issues of the day. And we had the ear of Carl D. Perkins, the same U.S. representative who held the hearings on the Scotia disaster in 1977. He also held hearings on the Topmost disaster in the spring of 1982, congressional hearings in Washington, DC. I flew up to DC with some of the widows. I was working with Davitt McAteer representing the widows and investigating the disaster, along with attorney Chip Yablonski, son of the slain UMWA reformer Jock Yablonski, and Tom Bethel, a regional journalist and former [VISTA] Appalachian Volunteer publicist. And the widows testified in front of Rep. Carl Perkins's congressional committee.

I had helped my clients prepare their statements, and Tom Gish printed our clients' testimonies verbatim in the *Mountain Eagle,* about three full pages of the newspaper, with each widow's story. I remember some of Eula Gibson's statement. She would talk like a typical coal miner's wife: "I don't know much about the mines. My husband wouldn't tell me much about them. He didn't want to scare me. I was pregnant with our first child. But I knew it was dangerous down there because James was looking for work at other locations. He didn't want to move until after the baby was born. But his clothing was so filthy with coal dust when he got home at night that I'd have to put it through the wash cycle at least two times to get it clean. Just once wouldn't do it. That's how I knew there was a lot of dust in that mine, and James would make comments from time to time. He was afraid of the dust, afraid there would be an explosion sometime."

So it was these very heartfelt testimonies from the widows about what their husbands had said to them that Tom Gish published in the *Mountain Eagle.* That's what fueled this widespread outcry for a public hearing. And we contacted the editors of other local newspapers. The *Troublesome Times* from Hindman, in Knott County, the *Floyd County Times,* the *Lexington Leader,* I believe, and the *Louisville Courier-Journal* all wrote good editorials calling for public hearings. We had a whole bunch of them. We had Sam Church, president of the United Mine Workers calling for a public hearing. We had some congressmen endorsing public hearings, state legislators. We had this great array of people saying public hearings are needed.

And the head of MSHA in 1982 was Ford Barney Ford, a Reagan appointee, formerly head of California OSHA. Reagan was your traditional Republican anti-regulation, "regulations are killing industry" type of president. And Ford B. Ford was anti-regulation-minded, as he had been in California and laid out what he called "compliance assistance,"—he would say, "We don't want our inspectors to be policemen, to go out to the mines and be confrontational." The theory was that all coal operators are good guys, and, "If you just give them a little assistance—compliance assistance—teach them how to comply with the law, they'll take your lead. So instead of going out to the mines and being confrontational and issuing all these citations, we want you to work with mine operators." This mind-set was the cornerstone of the Reagan administration's management of MSHA. And looking at the string of disasters that happened during Reagan's presidency, we deduced that being soft on compliance was one of the major reasons.

But we got a hold of Ford B. Ford anyway and asked him to come to Hazard, Kentucky, to meet the Topmost families. The MSHA office at the time was in a little strip mall in Hazard. And Mr. Ford came down to Hazard with his entourage of MSHA officials. I was there representing the families, and I went through and introduced everybody to Mr. Ford. "This is a widow, these are her children, this is her mother and dad—." We had this great lineup of people, and we presented Mr. Ford with this stack of petitions totaling about 11,000 signatures, explaining why we're asking for a public hearing. The press was there. Ralph Dunlop, the legendary reporter from the *Courier Journal*, was there. I think Lee Mueller from the *Lexington Herald-Leader* was there. Mr. Ford responded by announcing that he didn't think a public hearing would serve "any useful purpose." And therefore he declined the families' request to hold a public hearing.

So the next time Ford B. Ford was in Lexington speaking at a coal operators' convention, we were there picketing his speech outside. The widows were a strong presence. I remember one sign that said, "Eleven thousand people want hearings. Why doesn't Mr. Ford?" You know, that kind of thing, just letting him know and letting MSHA know that the families were not pleased, that in our view he was basically coddling the coal operators. We kept asking, "Why wouldn't you want to know why conditions had deteriorated to the point that a mine exploded and eight men were killed just trying to earn a living?" We had great public support for our position, but, you know, you can't force an agency to hold a public hearing. It just wasn't going to happen.

In representing some families of disasters at Topmost, followed by South Mountain eleven years to the day later, and the Kentucky Darby disaster, another secondary mine dust explosion in 2006, I've learned that the widows derive some sense of purpose out of advocating for mine safety for others after there's been a disaster. Of course they were devastated by the deaths of their own husbands, as well as by MSHA's response in the wake of the disaster. I've watched these women and their families in some cases for thirty-five years, all the way back to the Topmost disaster in 1981. I've seen Jamie Gibson, born two weeks after the disaster which killed her father, James, grow up, get married, and have children of her own. I've remained friends with April Slone. Her dad, Bobby Slone, was killed at Topmost. And Bobby had, I think, seven children with his wife, Ora, who was pregnant with their eighth child, and they were all left as orphans. April was about four at the time of the disaster. I've known her all these years. She's now an LPN [licensed practical nurse] and works over in Hazard. But you see the ongoing effects of children growing up without their dads and how devastating that is, how many lives it affects: not just the widow, not just the kid, but you have brothers and sisters, grandparents, any kin these workers had, and how it affects the community as a whole.

In the Kentucky Darby disaster on May 20, 2006—I'll just give one example—Roy Middleton was an electrician. And Kentucky Darby was a horrendous methane explosion. Two of the five miners who died were killed instantly because they were at the ignition point where the explosion occurred. But then there was carbon monoxide that spread throughout the mine and the other three miners died of carbon monoxide inhalation. They couldn't get out of the mine in time. And they had breathing devices that were supposed to provide fresh air for a period of time, which we don't think worked properly, because all of them still had fresh air left in their canisters when their bodies were found later.

So Roy Middleton was one of the miners who died of carbon monoxide inhalation. He had two daughters, young kids at the time, and I've maintained a friendship with the family. So I know that Danielle, the older daughter, became the valedictorian of Harlan County High School, and she went to the University of Kentucky on a full scholarship and is now in grad school. And the younger daughter, Natalie, a "Governor's Scholar," is still in high school. She's a high achiever like her sister. They were deprived of all the love and affection their father would have provided over the years, and you see how devastating it is long-term on the families, and, of course, the widows as well.

In the case of the Kentucky Darby disaster some of the miners who worked at the mine signed for me to become a miners' rep for the limited purpose of investigating the disaster. So I got to go into the Kentucky Darby mine for two days after the explosion and see all the devastation, all the destruction underground. The miners' bodies had been removed by that point, but MSHA and the Kentucky Department of Mines and Minerals granted me access because I was representing four of the widows and the one survivor, Paul Ledford.

Later we filed a lawsuit with Kellie Wilson as the local counsel. MSHA again did not hold a public hearing after the Kentucky Darby disaster. They reverted to a traditional, flawed process of calling people in and saying, "You have the right to refuse to answer any question, da-da, da-da." And because I was designated as a miners' rep I got to sit in on those interviews. Had I just been the attorney for the families, they would not have allowed me to sit in.

And every night after the proceedings, we would have a meeting with the families in Evarts, a small community near Holmes Mill, where the mine blew up, to meet with some of the widows at Melissa Lee's dog grooming parlor. And in this little store we would report to the families what everyone in the hearings had said during the interviews, which was very helpful, because typically after you have a mine disaster there's all kinds of rumors that spread through the community. We were actually able to report on exactly who had said what, which was significant because the women wanted to substantiate everything they could about why their husbands had been killed.

When I got to go underground as a miner's rep I told MSHA and the state I wanted to see the places where each of the miners' bodies had been found. So I was able to tell the widows, Mary Middleton, for example, here's where Roy's body was found on a map. This is how far he made it out of the mine before he was overcome by carbon monoxide poisoning. And even though that's very painful information, it was the details the women wanted to know.

Melissa Lee's husband, Jimmy Lee, for instance, was at the ignition source when the methane exploded. His body was thrown 120 feet. Of course miners underground have to wear hard hats.

It's required. And Jimmy Lee's hard hat was blown to bits. His wife wanted every piece back. She wanted every little scrap that she could get. They had two young sons, Seth and Ross, and two older ones by a previous relationship, Hayden and Brody, that Jimmy essentially was the dad for. And she was devastated, of course. All these fatherless children.

In the weeks and months that followed, a lot of widows wanted to speak out for mine safety, and like I was saying, it gives them a purpose. They know the devastation their family has gone through. They don't want other families to go through the same kind of loss.

So in 2007—I was in private practice by this time and working with the widows as well as my associates in the region—we lobbied the Kentucky General Assembly to pass a stronger mine safety law. We had already had the Sago disaster in West Virginia in January 2006, where twelve miners died. CNN gave that round-the-clock coverage, you know. They had announced at that disaster site that everybody had survived, only to discover that, no, only one person had survived. Twelve had perished. And just five months later in Harlan County we have the Kentucky Darby disaster.

So there had been an alarming number of mining deaths during that period and I was one of the "lobbyists" (and I use that term loosely), not a paid lobbyist, but working closely with the Appalachian Citizens' Law Center's attorney Wes Addington in Whitesburg and Steve Earle, the head UMWA official in Kentucky. In a draft of the bill I helped to formulate, we wrote in thirteen provisions that were stronger than those in the federal law—that *exceeded* the provisions in the federal law. So, for example, we wrote that the state agency had the authority to investigate any allegations of unsafe conditions, regardless of whether there was an accident or not. Therefore, any miner's complaint, any allegations, can be investigated by the State Department of Mines and Minerals. MSHA can't do that. They don't have the authority to subpoena people and have them come in. It's a failure of the Federal Mine Act.

But against all odds we were successful in our lobbying efforts. It was just a confluence of events. One was that we had widows testify. Melissa Lee testified. We had a widow, Stella Morris, her husband was killed near Cumberland in Harlan County on December 30, 2005. He was working underground and got his legs cut off by what's called a ram car. A ram car backed into him and cut off one leg and the other was pretty much severed and hanging by a thread. And we have in Kentucky what are called "METs," like an EMT in a medical situation.

But these Mine Emergency Technicians are specifically trained to help injured coal miners in case of a disaster or accident. But the law in Kentucky said you had to have one MET underground. And what happened in Bud Morris's case was that he got hit by one of these ram cars, and the MET turned out to be one of the mine owners. Well, we don't know exactly what happened, but the bottom line is the MET either panicked or, for whatever reason, did not treat Bud. He was the guy designated to treat the injured miners. He should have put a tourniquet on Bud's legs, elevated his legs, done other procedures. But instead he just left. He abandoned him. He walked off and never treated him. So you have a guy whose legs have been cut off, who's bleeding to death, left with coal miners who have had only rudimentary training, the annual training you have to take in first aid. And they tried to put a tourniquet on Bud's leg, but they didn't do it right. They didn't have all the materials they needed, and even though federal law requires that emergency materials be kept underground, they didn't have what they needed. The bottom line was they ended up putting Bud on a buggy to take him outside.

If you've ever been in a coal mine, you won't find smooth roads like driving down an interstate. They're rough and bumpy and full of holes, swags, and water. So you have a guy in extreme pain who's in and out of consciousness being taken out on a buggy, delirious, and they're hitting all these bumpy holes in the road. They finally got him outside. And in the end, no one treated him, and by the time an ambulance arrived and took him to the hospital he had died.

So in 2007, when we were trying to pass this law, our vision of it was based on common sense, you know, provisions that should have been the law anyway. And they were all written as a result of mining accidents in Kentucky in the last few years. So one of the new previsions called for *two* METs for every working shift underground. I mean, it just makes sense: What if the guy who's the MET gets hurt? Who's going to treat him?

As I said, there was a confluence of events that came together to pass that law. And one of the major reasons was because of miners' widows testifying. And so, for instance, Stella Morris, whose husband died when his legs got cut off, gave a very powerful, moving testimony in front of the committee considering the bill. She stood before the assembled hearing holding out the framed photo of her husband and talking about how his son Landen is going to grow up without knowing his father. He was an infant at the time his father was killed, and Landen said goodnight to the framed photo of his dad every night. Melissa Lee testified about her husband being killed in the Kentucky Darby explosion. Claudia Cole from Harlan County testified about her husband being killed pulling pillars in Harlan County. So those widows coming forward and speaking was really powerful.

The combination of widows' testimonials and timely editorials from the two major newspapers in Kentucky led to the passage of that bill. Amazingly, it passed the House and the Senate unanimously. Everybody voted for it. It was one of the rare victories for coal mine safety advocates in Kentucky, because the Kentucky

Coal Association was so powerful. And they were beside themselves, furious with the bill's passage.

When stringent laws are passed, like in the passage of the 1977 Mine Safety Act, the number of deaths has gone down. In 1983, for the first time in history, less than a hundred miners were killed. Thirty years later in 2014, sixteen miners died. But it was sixteen too many and devastating to the families involved. One of our clients, a widow, is waiting for state and national accident reports to be issued. Her husband, Mark Frazier, was killed in a mine over in Harlan County in March of this year. So it's three months later and we're still waiting for the reports.

Like most mining accidents—people talk about big disasters, which generate publicity, you know, the TV cameras, the newspaper reporting. But the reality is that most miners die one or two at a time, just like Mark Frazier did. When Bud Morris's legs were cut off, his death was the result of a single accident. And that's the reality of coal mining, particularly in Appalachia. You have a single miner killed here or there and it doesn't generate any publicity. Not that many people care about it. And there's no reform. But big disasters with multiple deaths offer opportunities to strengthen mine safety laws.

And what's infuriating to me about coal operators is that without exception, the National Mining Association and the Kentucky Coal Association have opposed every single piece of mine safety legislation that's been proposed over the past thirty-five years. But when the death toll is reduced *because of* the laws, then they want to take credit for it.

And that's why it's widely said, as our widows and orphans know so well, that all mine safety laws are written in the blood of coal miners.

Jack and the Coal Giant
Jack Spadaro as told to Michael and Carrie Kline

Carrie Kline and I got to sit in Jack's kitchen for a whole day and listen to this tale unfold. And now that we've heard it, it won't let us rest, for indeed, it's as good a Jack tale as was ever told. This time it's Jack telling of his own struggles with Old King Coal—Jack Spadaro, that is. Jack was a career federal mine inspector, born and bred in a coal mining town, who grew up in determined, personal pursuit of coal mine health and safety, and who pitted all of his charisma, wit, and persuasive gifts in efforts to protect and preserve the Appalachian Mountains and people he cherishes.

WEST VIRGINIA ITSELF—THE WHOLE STATE—IS 80 PERCENT forested, and it is the largest unbroken forest east of the Mississippi River, larger than even the Adirondacks and those forests in New England. West Virginia and parts of eastern Kentucky are the mother forests for all of North America. When the glaciers came the last time, 10,000 years ago, it scraped almost all the vegetation off the North American continent except in West Virginia and Kentucky. Because the glaciers came down to the Ohio River and stopped, West Virginia's forest remained intact. And from that forest, all the seed for all the rest of the forests in North America were generated; and so, this is the mother forest for North America.

And that's why I got involved in the fight against mountaintop removal way back in the 1970s when Bob Gates was first making his film *In Memory of the Land and the People*. And I've been involved ever since. Even though I was working for the government, I still did everything I could to control what was happening and at least try to protect some areas and also protect people who lived near these places.

After I got out of high school, I first worked for what later became the Mine Safety and Health Administration. It was an enforcement arm of the Bureau of Mines. I had intended to be an English major because I had a terrific high school English teacher named Eliza Park. She had come out of the coalfields of eastern Kentucky with her husband Bill Park, who was head of the Bureau of Mines in Mount Hope. I was getting to be a senior, and she came to me and said, "What are you going to do?" And I said, "Well, I'm going to be an English teacher, just like you."

She said, "I don't think that's a good idea. You are already a great writer, and you read, and you're literate. But you need to find a way to make a living. Your father's a janitor, and he doesn't make any money, and English teachers don't make any money. So, I suggest you go talk to my husband who runs the Bureau of Mines and see what he can offer you in the way of a cooperative program to go to college." So I did, and he said he needed mining engineers, and I was good in sciences, but I wasn't so sure about the Bureau of Mines. And he said, "Just give it a try."

And so I did. I started working the day after I got out of high school for the Bureau of Mines in 1966. And the first week I went to Buffalo Creek, West Virginia, and worked all summer there, so I got to know the place. I knew the people there, and I knew the miners. I knew the whole place thoroughly. I lived in a hotel room down in Man that summer, and so part of my training was just being there. In 1968, I was still on this training program. I'd go to school through the year, work in the summers for the Bureau of Mines. I went in the mines. I would tag along with inspectors down in the mines and learn mine safety and mine ventilation and everything about the mines.

So in the summer of 1968 I spent five weeks—all of August and the first part of September—in the Farmington mine traveling with an inspector. His name was Merle McManus, and he was the best inspector in northern West Virginia. He and I traveled that whole mine—every section of the mine. I walked all the escape ways. I took dust samples. I took air samples. We closed the mine twice because of excessive methane. McManus was a great inspector. He was right on it, and he told me after that inspection, "I'm afraid that one of these mines in northern West Virginia is going to blow up some day in a big way, because our regulations don't give us enough authority to really go after the problem. The operators are camouflaging the problems we're having with ventilation." They'd get in compliance to the last point that the inspectors could sample, and that was that. They didn't do anything beyond that.

So in November of '68, the Farmington mine exploded, and seventy-eight miners died. I was there when they were sealing the mine, and I was there when the smoke was coming up out of the Llewellyn shaft, and I was there with the widows and their children waiting, knowing that their husbands were dead but still waiting and hoping. So for the next year I was going around to all the seals and taking air samples and stuff. Because I had been in that mine and knew some of the men who were dead, it made mine safety really personal for me, and that's why I've done the work I've done.

I finished college in 1970 and worked for a while for a mining company in Fayette County. Allied Chemical Corporation had a mine in Harewood, near Montgomery, and I worked there underground. A year later I went back to West Virginia University and was teaching mining classes and doing research on acid mine drainage. That's when the Buffalo Creek dam failed, on February 26, 1972. So I was appointed by the dean of the School of Mines to do the engineering study on the dam failure, along with a team of people from the Bureau of Mines. I was twenty-three years old.

I got there in March to begin interviewing people who had survived, along with people who had knowledge about the dams and how they were built. I was going to do a history of the construction of the dams, but I had to get to some of the people in the valley who were now scattered amongst various HUD trailer parks. So, I began doing that, and I can remember those faces like it was last week. They had lost everything.

People had lost their homes. One woman had lost five members of her family. Others had lost cousins, aunts, uncles, immediate family members. I was so inexperienced. I had never seen or heard anything like this. I took notes, and then I compiled a list of people we needed to have come and testify. There were going to be a series of hearings by a commission that was appointed by the governor, and that's how I got involved. The governor had made the dean of the School of Mines the chairman of the committee, and the dean had asked me to do this work. He didn't come himself.

Fortunately, there were eight other commission members, and they were good people, honorable people, and so they let me do my job. And so, I went up and down the hollows to the remaining houses, and began piecing together the events. And then, in early April of 1972, we had our first hearing at the gymnasium at Man High School. I set up a tape recorder and recorded the hearing. There was a long line of folks who came to testify about what personally happened to them and all the events leading up to the dam failure.

We found that four years before, a woman from Buffalo Creek had written a letter to Governor Hewlett Smith. And the date of the letter was February 26, 1968, exactly four years to the day before the fatal event. She wrote, "There is a dam that is being built up here at the head of Buffalo Creek by Buffalo Mining, and we're all afraid that it is going to fail and kill us all." And she sent it to the governor. The governor sent it to the Public Service Commission and the Department of Natural Resources, and they all said, "Well yeah, there is a dam up there, but there is nothing we can do about it," because there were no laws governing that kind of construction at that time. So nobody did anything.

We also found that the federal agencies—Soil Conservation Service, U.S. Bureau of Mines—there were at least five government agencies who knew of the dam and that it was in really bad shape. None of them had acted. So, they had four years' warning.

And when we interviewed people, we found that they had counted on the word of a guy named Steve Dasovich, the head of Buffalo Mining, a subsidiary of Pittston Company at that time. And the morning of the dam failure, Dasovich had been up on the dam all night long, apparently, because he knew there were some problems with the dam. And he came down off the mountain and met with a group of people in the town of Saunders and told them, "Everything is okay. You can all go home." And the woman who lost all of her family did, and all of her family drowned. She was the only survivor.

And so, the residents of Buffalo Creek trusted these people who ran these mines to protect them. But they just put their trust in the wrong place, and, of course, that was the way it was in those towns in those times. The mining company pretty well called the shots for everybody. So, we found all this out in this series of hearings. But in particular on that day, it was so painful for me; I couldn't always focus on what they were saying, so I was counting on the recorder. And there were seven or eight more hearings.

And I continued, of course, interviewing people all throughout the spring and summer of '72. I can remember working all night writing the report. I can remember being just amazed. I had stacks of documents going all the way back into the 1950s that showed how the government, along with the mining company, had really created this disaster and allowed it to exist for a long time. In fact they built a series of dams on the site that were all unstable, and the third one they built on top of eighty feet of slurry that had been deposited by the previous two dams. Now, common sense tells you that's stupid, you know? So, when the dam failed, it was because it dissolved, essentially, in fifteen minutes. It had become so saturated and had such a weak foundation that it simply dissolved and then suddenly released 126 million gallons of coal slurry that was very much like a tsunami going seventeen miles down the Buffalo Creek Valley.

The woman, Mrs. Woodrum, who wrote the letter in February of 1968, had gone to the hillside after being warned, and the first thing she saw coming down the valley was her house on the crest of the tidal wave from the dam failure. And then later, I talked to ten-year-old Gail Ambergie, who lived up a side hollow that the wave went by. The flood didn't get up into her hollow. But when she went down from her house that morning, she found her favorite playmate from her grade school in the mud.

So, there were all those stories that have stuck with me all these years. And even though I've talked about the flood many times, it still shakes me up to remember it. The commission members debated about how we should reach our conclusions. I wrote all the technical part of the report on the history of the dam construction, but the commissioners and I together wrote the conclusions and recommendations.

It turned out that my boss, the dean of the School of Mines, was trying to protect the Pittston Company. That's why Arch Moore appointed him to run the commission. But the other eight members, including a guy named Sandy Latimer, a Republican and head of the Department of Natural Resources, stuck with me on the content of the report and the conclusions, and several others on the committee did the same. They were really good, honorable, professional people, and they insisted on writing a clean report.

Their first conclusion was that the Pittston Company was guilty of callous disregard for the welfare of the people downstream from the Buffalo Creek dam, and that this attitude toward the public is prevalent throughout the mining industry. It was a pretty powerful statement for a committee appointed by Arch Moore, the avowed friend of coal. Working with the other commissioners reinforced my belief that if one persists, you can actually get some good done with people, if they are honest and straightforward about what's really happening in the coalfields.

And so, in the arguments back and forth over the content of the report, the dean's sitting at the far end of the table, I'm sitting at this end, and he looks down the table at me. I was supposed to be on loan from West Virginia University. He looks down the table, and he says, "Spadaro, if you don't keep your mouth shut, you won't have a job tomorrow," and he meant my job back at the university.

And I said, "That's okay, I quit." I was twenty-three at the time, but I realized you could survive losing your job, an important lesson for me. So I quit. I didn't go back to WVU. But Sandy Latimer, who had supported me throughout the Commission hearing, gave me a job running the Dam Safety Division for the State of West Virginia because he knew I would do a good job.

Turned out there were many other dams, and then, there have been altogether a dozen or so fairly sizable failures. In October of 2000 in Martin County, Kentucky, there was a gully-whomper at a dam owned by Massey Energy. I was working for the Mine Safety and Health Administration at that time running the Mine Academy that trained all the federal mine inspectors, and we had a really good man running that agency. His name is Davitt McAteer, and he and I had been friends since the Buffalo Creek study, because we met during that time when he was working for Ralph Nader. A few years later, McAteer went to work as head of safety for the United Mine Workers of America.

He was originally from Fairmont and lost some of his people in the Farmington explosion in 1968. His family owned a local grocery store. So he knew some of the victims at Farmington and was also interested in what was happening with Buffalo Creek. McAteer was a graduate of Wheeling Jesuit University and WVU Law School. Later on he teamed up with the folks who formed the Miners for Democracy, after Jock Yablonski was murdered and Arnold Miller was running for president of the United Mine Workers. And Davitt later became the chief of safety in 1972 or '73 for the United Mine Workers and was there for five or six years, I think. He trusted me a lot, so when I was running the Mine Academy, he called me after the Martin County dam failure.

McAteer had appointed Tony Oppegard to run the investigation in Martin County, but he wanted me to run the engineering evaluation—the geotechnical investigation—where we drilled into the foundation area to find out what had happened, and what had caused the Martin County dam to fail. And I remember him saying really clearly, "I want you to go down there and tell me where we messed up."

So we started our investigation in October of 2000, had interviewed like thirty or forty people and had about thirty, forty more people to interview. And, of course, in November of 2000, George W. Bush and company stole the presidential election. By January 21, 2001, we were ordered to stop our investigation by the new Bush administration, which had just been inaugurated that day. And, of course, we didn't stop.

So they fired Tony Oppegard, who had headed up the investigation. They couldn't fire me because I was civil service. And so, we were told to wrap up the investigation: "You are not going to want to do any more investigation." And I said, "Hell, you know we're about ready to issue ten citations to this company for willful violations of the law, for lying on their application," and so forth. They said, "Oh no, you're not." And so, a few months went by, and a revised report was being drafted, and I refused to sign it. I told the guy who replaced Oppegard that I wasn't going to sign it. So, he called the newly appointed head of the Mine Safety and Health Administration (MSHA), David Lauriski, and told him I wasn't going to sign it. Well, they wanted my name on it to give it credibility, and I said, "No. You haven't investigated this thing, you're covering it up, and I promise you, I am going to tell the world about it. There is no way in hell I am going to sign that report."

Lauriski called me again and asked me one more time to sign, and I said, "I am not signing the report. I never will sign the report." And I then was contacted by a reporter from Salon.com, who did a long interview with me about why I wouldn't sign the report and my claim that the government was covering up the true causes of the dam failure. I had found that six years before the dam had failed, the bottom had dropped out of the reservoir and the slurry had drained into an underground coal mine and leaked out into a couple of creeks down in Martin County. They plugged the hole, but they kept on using the reservoir. The MSHA allowed them to keep doing it for six more years.

And then by October of 2000, the impoundment was full enough of slurry that it punched another hole through the bottom and unleashed 300 million gallons of coal slurry into Coal Water Creek, which flooded into Wolf Creek, the Big Sandy River, and the Ohio River and killed everything a hundred miles downstream. It wiped out seventeen public town water supplies. And so I wasn't going to let it pass, because I had sworn way back in 1972 that I wasn't going to stand by and watch another government cover-up happen to allow the government and the company to get by with such deliberate violations of the law.

So I talked to the press and kept talking, and I wrote letters to the inspector general for the Department of Labor. And finally—I think it took a couple years—but finally the Bush administration decided they had enough of me, and I was called to Washington for a meeting. And while I was there, they came in and changed the locks on the doors to my office at the Academy and confiscated all my files on the Martin County coal slurry spill and brought charges against me that were later determined to be unfounded— and tried to fire me.

And that's when I *really* went public. I went to the *New York Times* and then to *60 Minutes* to tell Bob Simon and the world that the Bush administration was "the most corrupt administration in regard to mine safety that I had ever seen in my lifetime and that they were deliberately covering up the culpability of the government, as well as the responsibility of Massey Energy." And I remember saying to Bob Simon that Massey Energy was "misrepresenting the facts." He said, "What's the difference between misrepresenting the facts and lying?" And I said, "They were lying. Yes, that's right." (Laughs)

So that did not endear me to the Bush administration. Finally, after about a year and a half of haggling back and forth, I simply retired.

I had just been forced out of the government. I had been working in the government for thirty years and had had a pretty distinguished career, and so I was really kind of down in the dumps. I think I had all of maybe 200 dollars in the bank and wasn't sure exactly how things were going to go financially in the future, and I was—I was down. You know? My only purpose in raising the alarm about this investigation was to make certain that the mining company and the agencies responsible for enforcing mine health and safety and environmental laws be held accountable for their failure to do so. More than one hundred miles of stream were polluted by the Martin County coal slurry spill. All life forms in and along the streams and rivers were obliterated. Thousands of people were affected.

When I objected to weakened investigation reports and less than appropriate enforcement actions, I was immediately attacked by administrators in the Labor Department appointed by the Bush administration. But the public support for my stance against a whitewash of the Martin County spill was overwhelming, and eventually, the Bush administration had to back down on its efforts to fire me. Many have offered unwavering support and continue to believe that a better world is possible: Vivian Stockman from the Ohio Valley Environmental Coalition, members of the Coal River Mountain Watch, the West Virginia Environmental Council, the Sierra Club, Kentuckians for the Commonwealth, and the United Mine Workers of America, to name but a few.

The fact remains, however, that Massey Energy, the company responsible for the spill, and which has the sorriest environmental record in Appalachia and a terrible mine health and safety record, has gotten away with its negligence because the corporate executives have direct access and influence with top officials of the Mine Safety and Health Administration and other government agencies with authority over mining operations.

Massey Energy contributed $100,000 to the National Republican Senatorial Committee while it was being investigated for the Martin County coal slurry spill. I could go on. It is better for me to say simply that from my experience and from the experience of others who have spoken publicly, the Bush administration is one of the most corrupt, lawless, and dangerous governments that this country has ever seen. In the past several years, I have seen the most callous disregard for the welfare of workers and their families that I have witnessed in my thirty-six years of work in the coalfields of Appalachia. The people of the Appalachian coal mining regions are being confronted daily with life-threatening situations such as landslides and flooding that are caused by mountaintop removal operations. They have no control over this situation and few options to escape.

I said earlier that I had taken an engineering degree and became a social worker, when I first went to West Virginia University. Even though I enrolled in an engineering program, I did one of these aptitude tests that find out what you really want to do, and I scored the lowest on engineering and the highest on social work, like 80–90 percent on social work and 10 percent on engineering. So I figured I was in the wrong major, but I went ahead and stuck with it because I had a lot of scholarships.

Over time I was able to take that knowledge of engineering and use it, not only when I was working for the government, but since then, working as an expert witness on behalf of plaintiffs in lawsuits involving flooding and mine damage and mine subsidence and giving them a voice, because most of the people who have knowledge in these fields work for the industry and reflect the industry point of view.

Upon leaving the government I spent a long time here on the mountain. I didn't go anywhere much for about a year and a half. I was pretty tired. But after a few months of feeling sorry for myself, I decided to start working again. So by March of 2005 I was being hired as an expert witness in mine safety cases where miners had been injured or killed. And unfortunately, because of the terrible policies of the Bush administration and the failure to enforce mine safety laws, there were lots of accidents and some terrible mine disasters, beginning in January of 2006 at Sago in northern West Virginia. I was hired by a really fine attorney out of Morgantown named Al Karlin to work on the investigation of the Sago disaster and serve as his expert witness.

And then later came another disaster—a mine fire in Aracoma in Logan County—and I wasn't as directly involved with that, but I was still involved. And then later that year—in Harlan County, Kentucky, the Darby mine, where five miners were killed in an explosion—I was hired by Tony Oppegard to work on that case as an expert. And again, in 2007 at Crandall Canyon in Utah, I wasn't hired as an expert, but I was able to comment about that disaster on MSNBC.

I said that, once again, the disaster, the death of those men rested partly on the shoulders of the administrators of the Mine Safety and Health Administration (MSHA), who had been appointed by President Bush, and that it was the lax enforcement and the failure to enforce the mine safety standards regarding roof control that led to the initial mine burst that killed the first six miners.

And then later, there were three rescue workers who were killed because the owner of the mine, Bob Murray, took over the rescue operations, and the MSHA leadership acquiesced and allowed him to and let one of their own inspectors go in there and be killed, even though they knew that six miners who were already there had died. They risked these other people's lives and killed three of them. So they killed nine people altogether. I said that Murray and the leadership of the MSHA were responsible for the murders of these miners and should be held accountable. And the great thing about that was I wasn't working for the government anymore, and I could say whatever the hell I wanted.

So then along came after that, of course, the Upper Big Branch disaster in 2010, and I was hired by a team of lawyers to represent several families as an expert witness. I went into that mine and walked all over it, crawled across the longwall face, and became pretty intimate with the layout. The signs of the force of the explosion were everywhere. The bent plates on the roof bolts, the destroyed overcasts, all the stoppings in the mine had been blown out. The explosion was so powerful it exploded in one direction and then exploded again, and the force came back in the other direction. It killed everything and destroyed the entire structure—the ventilation structure of the mine as far away as two and a half miles from the ignition site.

And that could only have happened with the failure of the mine operator to adequately rock dust the mine and with a deliberate neglect of the basic principles for mine ventilation and preventing explosions. And that was later borne out in the MSHA official report and the report authored by, actually, Beth Spence and Davitt McAteer and others on an investigative team that had been appointed by the governor. And then finally, in the conviction of Don Blankenship this past year for creating conditions that allowed such dangers to exist.

In early May of 2016, Don Blankenship went to prison for conspiring to circumvent the mine health and safety laws. But he is only going to spend a year in jail, and that is because the crime of deliberately circumventing the mine safety regulations is only a misdemeanor. It was written into the law by certain coal country senators, like Wendell Ford. They wrote weakened penalties for deliberately violating mine safety laws to protect mine operators from this kind of prosecution. The crimes that Blankenship would have been spending more time in jail for were crimes against money—crimes against Securities Exchange Commission regulations—which could have gotten him as much as thirty years. So that says something about this country. We penalize somebody for crimes against money more severely than we penalize them for killing people. This is Wendell Ford's legacy.

More recently, I have been able to be involved in a lawsuit against the owner of mines in southern West Virginia who has contaminated groundwater. He runs surface mining operations in which acid mine drainage seeps into groundwater systems and contaminates wells of families that have been there for generations. One woman in her late seventies had lived in the house for forty-six years, had good quality water until the mining operation carved up the mountain above her. She now has 500 times the safe level of arsenic in her water well. She can't drink her water.

So that's what the case was about. There were sixteen families altogether.

But we lost the case because the jury decided that they didn't want to do anything that would jeopardize jobs in the coalfields. So they ruled in favor of the mining company. The jury was persuaded that the most important thing for all of us is for somebody to have a job, regardless of whether it contaminates somebody's water or not, regardless of whether it creates unsafe conditions for the public. Jobs are paramount, and that's been the problem all along in these years that I have worked.

Most often we've found in the mining industry, a constant pressure to produce coal at all costs, and that's what happened at Upper Big Branch. That's what happened at Sago. That's what happened at Aracoma. In all of those places where miners have been killed or maimed, we generally find the mine management has failed to implement safety procedures or take the time to provide safe equipment or install the safety features that need to be installed to protect workers, and that production is paramount. These operator failures are generally referred to as "accidents." But there are no accidents in the mines, really.

And that's gone on throughout the history of the industry. That's what the Buffalo Creek Commission wrote, that Pittston had shown "callous disregard for the welfare of people in the community" and that this attitude is prevalent throughout the industry. That was in 1972, and here we are in 2016, and the same attitude from the industry prevails. The coal industry has never given anything other than jobs to these communities. They degraded the water, polluted the environment. They have put miners at risk. Miners have been maimed or killed by the thousands—tens of thousands in these coalfields.

And if you go to McDowell County, West Virginia, it's the poorest county in West Virginia. It's had one and a half billion—one and a half *billion* tons of high-grade metallurgical coal taken from the ground, from around 1890 until now. It was the best coal you could find, the Pocahontas Seam, the very best, most expensive coal. It was the coal that sold for three hundred dollars a ton in its heyday. McDowell is still the leading coal-producing county in United States industrial history. And it's the poorest county in the state today and one of the poorest counties in the whole country.

Andrew Carnegie, his companies, mined coal there to make steel. Andrew Carnegie didn't leave a library in McDowell County, as in many of his other industrial fiefdoms. He didn't even leave a book. There is nothing there from Carnegie and U.S. Steel, which made fortunes over the years mining McDowell coal to make steel. The population has dwindled from roughly 110,000 people in the early 1950s to around 25,000 people today, and a good half of those people are unemployed now, so the industry didn't give a thing to the communities that nurtured it. It didn't give a thing to the people who mined its coal, except now some of them have black lung compensation, if they're lucky, if they found a good lawyer and then fought their way through a bureaucratic maze to get it.

So a hundred and fifty years of coal mining in West Virginia hasn't done that much good for the people living—and dying—here. The attitude of the industry has been entirely to extract and exploit. I have not seen one coal mine operator—even a locally owned coal operator—show genuine concern for long-term benefits to the people who mined their coal. Not once. I would have gladly exalted somebody who did that, but I have not seen any of them do it. It's never proven true. The wealth goes away. There's no reinvestment in the community. There isn't even a four-lane highway in McDowell County. There's nothing. The school built on top of an abandoned strip mine is cracking because the ground is unstable. There's never been a plan by the industry or the government of West Virginia to capture some of that wealth and have it remain where it was made. It just hasn't happened. So more mining now is not going to do any good because, historically, it has done little to nothing to benefit people in the region over the long term.

There is short-term benefit from some jobs, and the industry was a huge employer in southern West Virginia. There's no question. But if you go to all those towns now, Mullens, Welch, Logan, Williamson, and smaller towns, they're dying because the economy is crashing, coal is dwindling, and the demand is diminishing especially for steam coal for coal-fired power plants. It's not because of government policies or regulations. Most power producers are now converting their coal-fired power plants to natural-gas-fired power plants because it is only about one-third the cost of mining and transporting coal to the power plant. So we are in a serious economic decline.

I would love to see the kind of development in the southern coalfields that's happened in northern West Virginia to create other industries related to the information technology world. Southern West Virginia could have stimulated those kinds of developments with seed money and other incentives a long time ago, but it was never done. There was no substitute economy, ever. My hometown, Mount Hope, is virtually empty now because the New River Coal Company mined all the coal that it owned. It's over. And when I grew up there in the 1950s and '60s, every storefront was full. There was something there for everyone.

The long-term investments it takes to create other industries were never made by the mining industry or local governments. We have never had any decent leadership in West Virginia that embraced inevitable change in energy sources. And even Senator Byrd, when he finally began to realize what was happening with coal, it was too late, and he was dying, and it was over. And Jay Rockefeller, who was one of the more progressive governors, spoke of it at the end of his career, but it was too late. He didn't have his power anymore. He couldn't muster any support for new ideas if he had thought of any.

So none of these entrenched politicians took the initiative to create different kinds of economies in the coalfields. Not once. And unfortunately, the working coalfield residents who have been looking to those kinds of leaders all these years haven't understood the link between the coal industry and power brokers who determine public policy. So now the rank-and-file voters are still embracing more false prophets who promise them the return of coal jobs that are simply not going to happen.

Coal miners are choosing in mid-2016 to believe that someone running for office at the governor's level can restore the coal industry and give everybody jobs again. I'm really feeling great sorrow, actually, that so many people have bought into these lies.

You can see it clearly in some of the interviews that have been done with coal miners who have been laid off or who are about to be laid off. They simply don't want to change the way they live. They don't want to change their work. They're satisfied with what they had, and so they're not willing to take the risk in learning a new technology and a new way of making a living. They've always been able to count on it: if their father worked in the mine, they would work in the mine. That's not going to happen anymore, and it's uncomfortable for them. It's what makes them so angry. They have to change, and people often resist that change.

It's not going to happen the way the politicians "promise" because there is simply not the demand for coal now due to the low cost of natural gas. And there are going to be other alternative energy sources later. There will still be a pretty steady demand for metallurgical-grade coal for making steel from southern West Virginia. And that market should come back up in the next year or two.

But at the same time, these folks who have been employed for all these years in mining need to realize that they've got to change the way they live and think if they're going to survive and have their families prosper. They need to look for and build a new economy that is more in tune with the national economy now—like the growth in the information technology industry, which has happened in northern West Virginia—in Clarksburg, in Fairmont, and in Morgantown. Actually, Monongahela County has a very low unemployment rate, I think about 3.2 percent, and that's because they've built a new industry that's tied to learning new technologies and ultimately alternative energy sources.

West Virginia has land now that has been flattened from mountaintop removal that could probably easily be converted to either wind power or solar power. There's a vast area near here that was leveled by Hobet Mining that could be used for solar power, I'm certain. And then simply other industries can be pursued in these areas where people are still clinging to the idea that they can go back to their old way of life.

I think it's really unfortunate that no one in the leadership of our state or region did anything to develop new IT industries in southern West Virginia and eastern Kentucky, where there was a workforce that could be trained. For instance, the air-conditioning and heating system in my house was installed by a former coal miner, who was an electrician in the mines, so he had technical knowledge. He got laid off, he went to school and learned how to do installations for air-conditioning and heating, and he's made a good living as an independent contractor doing that, actually, more money than working as an electrician in the mines.

I just recently got a proposal from another electrician who had worked at this Hobet mine. He's retired now, and he's starting a generator business. He tells me he's got an enormous amount of business—more business than he knows what to do with. So, there are alternatives, and we need to really work on those as an innovative community.

It's ironic that China is leading us in alternative energy development. At the same time, they are using a lot of coal-fired power plants. But they've seen, as a nation, what the future is, and I think now, because of the new policies implemented by the Obama administration, we're headed in the right direction.

But we've had these resistant forces in the fossil fuels industry stonewalling it for years, this kind of progress, because they make a lot of money holding us hostage to their supply of energy that is controlled entirely by them. Their resistance to considering new possibilities is driven by the fear that it would be harder to control energy if people had available to them solar panels and other affordable energy alternatives.

An Appalachian writer who understood this pretty well was a very dear friend of mine. His name was James Still and he lived in Hindman, Kentucky. I met him at the Hindman Writers' Workshop in 1980. Poems he wrote decades ago deal with the issues of the extractive industry and its corrosive intrusion on rural workers, traditional values, and landscapes. In closing I'll share this from James Still's *Wolfpen Poems*:

Heritage

I shall not leave these prisoning hills
Though they topple their barren heads to level
    earth
And the forests slide uprooted out of the sky.
Though the waters of Troublesome, of Trace Fork,
Of Sand Lick rise in a single body to glean the
    valleys,
To drown lush pennyroyal, to unravel rail fences;
Though the sun-ball breaks the ridges into dust
And burns its strength into the blistered rock
I cannot leave. I cannot go away.

Being of these hills, being one with the fox
Stealing into the shadows, one with the new-born
    foal,
The lumbering ox drawing green beech logs to mill,
One with the destined feet of man climbing and
    descending,
And one with death rising to bloom again, I cannot
    go.
Being of these hills I cannot pass beyond.

—James Still

Modern Battles

Nathan J. Fetty

Nathan J. Fetty is a public interest lawyer from central West Virginia whose family has many generations of roots in the state. An avid student of Appalachian history and politics, he concentrates his legal work in areas of coal mine health and safety, environmental protection, and consumer rights.

IN CENTRAL APPALACHIA, IT'S NOT USUALLY POLITICALLY, so-cially, financially, or professionally advantageous to talk about the downsides of polluting and extractive industry. The same industries that cause so many problems also have driven local economies. If you don't work in coal mining, oil and gas, or tim-ber, or similar industries—or somehow rely on those industries for a livelihood—chances are you're related or close to someone who does. It's often heretical to raise concerns about how those industries operate, or attempt a discussion about what happens when those industries move on.

But truths are truths, even if they're difficult to say or hear. The coal industry is on the ropes. Just as national and global eco-nomic forces spurred the coal industry to prominence through the twentieth century, such forces are ushering in the industry's demise. Coal is falling out of favor, with escalating worldwide attention to climate change and coal's role in accelerating it. Global finance giants such as JPMorgan Chase, Bank of America, Citigroup, and Morgan Stanley are retreating from funding ar-rangements involving the coal industry. Regulators at all levels are encouraging—even compelling—other sources of energy. In particular, natural gas produced by hydrofracturing methods— with its own suite of workplace and environmental concerns and community impacts—is supplanting coal as a power-generating fuel. In fact, in March 2016, for the first time in history, natural gas was set to generate more power in the United States than coal.[1] Incentives for renewable energy and energy efficiency may well be on an uptick.[2]

In that same month, Oregon Governor Kate Brown signed legislation to phase out use of out-of-state coal by that state's two biggest energy producers. The implication, of course, is that perhaps other states (and nations?) will follow suit. Stock prices for nearly all major coal producers have plummeted. The world's largest private coal company, Peabody Energy, has gone bankrupt. Arch Coal, the country's second-largest coal producer, filed for bankruptcy in January 2016. Arch's stock had traded five years prior to its bankruptcy at $260 per share, but traded at less than $1 per share at the time of its bankruptcy. Arch's bankruptcy followed those by coal giants Alpha Natural Resources, Patriot Coal, and Walter Energy. Other coal producers seem to have seen the writing on the wall and are scaling back or getting out of the coal business. For example, Consol Energy, Inc. and its predecessor companies had been a fixture in the coal industry for over a century, but in 2013 it offloaded five northern West Virginia underground coal mines, some of the country's largest.

It's worth backing up to trace the arc of modern battles involving this contentious industry.

Turmoil and Reform within the United Mine Workers of America

The tumult within—and because of—the coal industry never really abated after the early violent unionization battles and the UMWA's rise to prominence through the middle of the twentieth century. It just took a variety of new (and not so new) forms.

After legendary UMWA president John L. Lewis's death, the UMWA leadership took a series of corrupt twists and turns through the 1960s. The UMWA's infamous president during that era was Tony Boyle. Boyle clashed with insurgent UMWA leader Jock Yablonski and eventually defeated him in an election for the UMWA presidency. Yablonski challenged the election results. While the battle for the UMWA leadership continued, Yablonski and his wife and daughter were murdered in their beds on New Year's Eve 1969. Boyle eventually was convicted and imprisoned for ordering hit men to carry out these murders. A movement within the UMWA, Miners for Democracy, was born of the Yablonski murders. This movement, populated largely by younger miners, organized and elected new leadership of the UMWA in 1972.

Devastation on Buffalo Creek

Aside from struggles within the miners' union, the Buffalo Creek disaster, a flood resulting from the failure of a series of Pittston Coal Company coal slurry dams on February 26, 1972, decimated sixteen communities in Logan County, West Virginia, killed 125 people and injured hundreds of others, left thousands of people homeless, and made an indelible psychological mark on the region. Sociologist Kai T. Erikson, in a seminal book about the disaster, documented its aftermath. He quoted one resident as saying:

> People here are not like they used to be. Only people who were in the flood realize that it's not rudeness when you have to ask them to repeat something simply because you weren't listening, your mind was somewhere else. Or you forget to ask them to come back again when they leave after a visit. Or, as happens every day, you start to say something and forget what it was, or just walk away while someone is still talking to you. Or you start looking for

something you know you have and then remember,
"That was before."[3]

To add insult to injury, Pittston officials declared that the disaster was an "Act of God" because the dam simply was incapable of holding the water that God poured into it. West Virginia's governor at the time, Arch A. Moore, will be long remembered for his mishandling of the disaster. In light of national media attention, and with a deaf ear to the families and communities that had been ripped apart, Moore famously lamented, "The only real sad part is that the state of West Virginia has taken a terrible beating that is worse than the disaster."[4] And although the state sued Pittston for $100 million for cleanup costs and other damages, Moore settled the state's claims for a paltry $1 million. Ever one with a questionable relationship to the coal industry, in 1990, Moore pleaded guilty to five felonies arising from extortion of money from an energy company for his reelection campaigns and then obstruction of the investigation into those activities. He served three years in federal prison and home confinement. Moore, a lawyer, also was disbarred.

Sadly, mine disasters are nothing new. The explosion of Consolidation Coal's No. 9 Farmington Mine in northern West Virginia in November 1968 killed seventy-eight miners. Politicians and UMWA leadership took to the national airwaves to defend the company and speak about how such disasters are inevitable in the industry. Only four decades later was the full truth revealed, when journalists and historians turned up evidence that the safety alarm on a ventilation fan at the No. 9 mine was disabled. As such, when this fan stopped working, the miners inside the mine were not alerted and thus did not withdraw from the mine as they ordinarily should have. The implication here is that scores of miners suffered deaths that could have been avoided.[5]

Fighting for Health and Safety

With disasters like the one at Farmington and coal miners' occupational illnesses seemingly commonplace, reforms to improve miners' health and safety became paramount for rank-and-file miners. Grassroots efforts—organizing, demonstrations, marches, strikes—gave a powerful voice to those miners who felt that UMWA and political leadership were ignoring them. Medical providers such as the legendary Drs. Donald Rasmussen and I.E. Buff began making—and speaking loudly about—the connection between miners' workplace exposure to respirable dust and deadly, incurable coal workers' pneumoconiosis (black lung).

These efforts eventually led to the 1969 passage of the Federal Coal Act (one year after the Farmington disaster) and then later the 1977 passage of the Federal Mine Act, the aim of which was to improve workplace health and safety conditions for the nation's miners. The Mine Act proclaims at its outset that "the first priority and concern of all in the coal or other mining industry must be the health and safety of its most precious resource—the miner." This legislation implemented a number of sweeping requirements to better miners' working conditions: inspections of workplaces, limits for respirable dust, a system of citations and enforcement actions against outlaw coal operators, mechanisms to improve health and safety regulations as knowledge and technology develop, protections for miners against backlash and punishment by their employers when those miners raise health and safety concerns, and the like.

While the Mine Act has been beneficial for the nation's miners, its administration and enforcement are far from perfect, and disasters and deadly illness still persist. Since 1968, nearly 80,000 miners have died from black lung. And the problem endures. For example, public health researchers in recent years have highlighted that advanced forms of miners' lung disease are appearing in startling numbers, even in relatively young miners. This is despite the Mine Act's mandate that federal regulators write and enforce rules to prevent miners' lung disease. In 1995, the National Institute for Occupational Safety and Health (NIOSH), a gem among otherwise often inert government bureaucracies, highlighted in a report that black lung and similar illnesses were on the rise and found that permissible levels of miners' exposure to coal dust should be cut in half.[6] Federal regulators at the Mine Safety and Health Administration (MSHA), an arm of the Department of Labor, have the authority and duty to write more protective health and safety regulations when the science supports such movement. But even in light of NIOSH's findings, MSHA sat on its hands for years. This author brought a lawsuit against the federal Department of Labor to compel lowering the respirable dust limit, but lost on a procedural (not substantive) point.

Since that time, NIOSH has continued its important work. Based on continued research and testing by the agency, NIOSH produced a report in 2014 showing that the rates of an advanced form of black lung—progressive massive fibrosis—were as prevalent among Appalachian coal miners as they were before the Coal Act and the Mine Act were enacted.[7]

There are several hypotheses among workplace health and safety advocates for why there is such a resurgence of this disease: cheating as to the results of data gathered from miners' personal dust monitors, mining of thinner seams of coal such that mining equipment cuts into strata containing more dangerous dust, longer working shifts, declining unionization and the knowledge and protection a unionized workplace provides, and technological developments of more powerful and more dust-generating mining equipment.

In early 2014, the Obama administration's MSHA finally proposed a regulation to dial back the amount of respirable dust to which coal miners are permitted to be exposed. The regulation also would require better monitoring and sampling of respirable dust. As is the case with virtually every effort to more tightly regulate the industry and protect miners, several coal industry trade groups and companies sued to stop the regulation. As of this writing, the industry challenge is pending.

Threats to the Mine Workers Union

If there is a pinpoint of the UMWA's greatest modern challenge, it may well be the Pittston strike of the late 1980s and early 1990s. Giving rise to this battle was the Pittston Company's decision to stop paying into a benefits trust for retired and disabled miners and their widows, as well as an increase in miners' health insurance costs and in hours required for miners to work without overtime pay. In April of 1989, UMWA members began striking across three states—Virginia, West Virginia, and Kentucky.

Union miners and their supporters sought to compel Pittston to negotiate a contract to restore such benefits. Epic measures ensued by strikers and others to slow production by the nonunion replacements. Pro-union protesters, sometimes assembling by the hundreds for individual actions, blocked coal trucks and slowed the pace of getting coal to market. While union supporters often employed nonviolent tactics, violence and threats of violence erupted on both sides. As the strike continued over the summer of 1989, tens of thousands of protesters from across the country joined in the Pittston strike. This elevated the strike on the national stage, attracting attention and support from figures like Jesse Jackson and César Chávez. The strike culminated with a nonviolent action in September 1989, when dozens of union workers engaged in a surprise sit-down strike at the Moss 3 preparation plant in Russell County,

Virginia, Pittston's main coal processing facility. This strike last-ed for four days, spurring attempts by the federal Department of Labor to broker a compromise.

Eventually, the UMWA and Pittston hatched a new con-tract restoring the benefits the strikers sought. The UMWA and Pittston entered into this new contract in early 1990, with both sides having taken a financial toll from the strike. The UMWA was able to claim victory here, but in the long run many Pittston operations eventually were sold to nonunion operators.

Blankenship's Rise

Aside from the challenges of the Pittston strike, the UMWA early on locked horns with a singular figure who looms large in the Appalachian coal industry: Donald L. Blankenship. Blankenship gained notoriety as an industry executive during a heated mid-1980s strike by the UMWA against Rawl Sales & Processing, an A.T. Massey Coal Co. subsidiary operating in southwestern West Virginia and eastern Kentucky. Massey, long an antiunion operation, attempted to break the union by operating its subsid-iaries "independently" of one another. The upshot is that Massey would attempt to reopen each subsidiary as nonunion. As such, the UMWA faced a multitude of smaller challenges on multiple fronts, which added up to a fundamental challenge to the heart of the union's operations.

Massey operations attempted to compel strikers to return to work only as nonunion workers, and under conditions different from (and less attractive to workers than) terms of employ-ment hatched under previous union contracts. Massey, notably, brought in armed guards to the site of strikes—an alarming throwback to coal operators' heavy-handed union-busting efforts in the early twentieth century. Massey also was not above shut-tering some of its operations rather than employing organized workers. Blankenship was able to ascend the Massey corporate ladder in large part because of his union-busting approach with the UMWA.

After such a colossal series of battles with coal operators, the UMWA emerged victorious but a little battered. Union membership numbers continued to decline as members aged and as hostile coal operators began paying wages competitive with those paid in organized workplaces. In this author's observation, as an attorney who has represented miners in health and safety matters, this was an effective company tactic. Younger miners, needing to provide for families and maybe not as appreciative as they should be about longer-term health and safety matters, often jumped at the chance to work for wages more on par with higher union wages. As the UMWA's stature declined, so did the industry-wide workplace health and safety benefits it conferred. Miners at nonunion operations found themselves without the backstop of, say, a union safety committee in their workplace.

A new generation of miners has come of age without the same union traditions as their forebears (and often with a West Virginia public education that downplays coal industry exploitation of the land and people.) They often are unaware of their workplace health and safety rights or, if they are, do not have an effective way to exercise them in the absence of a union safety net. Jobs are scarce and nonunion miners often are loath to "rock the boat."

Mountaintop Removal—Unprecedented Destruction
Just as there have been modern coal industry battles fought by workers within the industry, there have been raging battles resulting from the industry's abuses visited on the environment and communities where it operates. No issue epitomizes this battle more than mountaintop removal mining and its associated valley fills.

Surface mining—"strip-mining"—has always been contro-versial. The early "shoot and shove" strip jobs of the mid-twen-tieth century sparked outrage in the communities where the practice led to floods, landslides, and other tragedies. Traditional underground coal miners often distanced themselves from the "strippers." Coalfield citizens fought long and hard for federal protections, and eventually won passage of the federal Surface Mining Control and Reclamation Act (SMCRA, pronounced SMACK-ruh) in 1977. SMCRA established the primary enforce-ment scheme to reign in the coal industry's abuses of the envi-ronment and human communities.

In the run-up to SMCRA's passage, coalfield activists nearly succeeded in outlawing strip-mining altogether. However, with assurances that strip-mining would be tightly regulated and large-scale surface mines would be the exception rather than the rule (and leave behind a land-based asset that would lead to help-ful community development once the coal wealth was extracted), those "at the table" compromised to allow for limited, controlled strip-mining.[8]

Mountaintop removal is but one, albeit the most controver-sial, form of strip-mining. In mountaintop removal, operators blast and bulldoze away mountaintops to expose seams of coal. In the process, operators use millions of pounds of explosives. Then, using multistory draglines and other gargantuan equipment, they shove the "overburden" into adjacent hollows to create valley fills. Valley fills snuff out headwater streams (and all aquatic life in them), which are critical for the overall health of Appalachian river systems. At the bottom of the valley fills, buried under mil-lions of tons of mining rubble, are rich topsoil, timber, and other components of a diverse and productive temperate hardwood forest. The practice leaves behind thousands of acres of vast, barren landscapes of little or no use to adjacent communities. Surface and groundwater supplies are decimated, never to be restored. In West Virginia alone, hundreds of miles of streams have been destroyed.

As mountaintop removal (a term ensconced in SMCRA) came under scrutiny, the industry successfully deployed the term "mountaintop mining" as a public relations move to blunt public criticism and salve negative public perceptions. However, "mountaintop removal" has long been the term which the law, the industry, and regulators use to describe the practice—and an apt term it is.

Ironically, mountaintop removal and other forms of large-scale strip-mining became more common in the early to mid-1990s with the passage of amendments to the Clean Air Act in 1990. Those amendments incentivized production of cleaner burning, low-sulfur coal. As such, coal production shifted from higher-sulfur coal in northern West Virginia to low-sulfur coal in southern West Virginia, eastern Kentucky, western Virginia, and eastern Tennessee. At the same time, technological advances in the development of machinery allowed mountaintop removal to proliferate.

With that proliferation came environmental and community devastation unparalleled in the Appalachians. Coalfield citizens and organizations, backed into a corner and rebuffed by the legislative and executive branches of government, turned to the courts to reign in the problems from deforestation, flooding, blasting, dust, and noise. Innovative, dogged lawyers brought legal challenge after legal challenge. Scientists, engineers, economists, and other experts entered the fray to highlight and explain how mountaintop removal decimated forests, watersheds, communities, and long-term economic health.

Early victories were few and sometimes short-lived. Victories in the courts often resulted in legislative and executive attempts, sometimes successful, to undo those victories. However, with the nonprofit law firm Appalachian Mountain Advocates leading the way, mountaintop removal opponents seized on coal operations' Clean Water Act violations to hold operators accountable for foisting their costs of doing business onto the surrounding environment and communities. Particularly, challengers of mountaintop removal highlighted how water downstream from these operations often was polluted with toxic selenium. They also have shown how some such operations are responsible for high levels of conductivity downstream, which is an indicator of an unhealthy water body. As a result, coal operators have had to install expensive treatment technologies to deal with such water pollution, making mining prohibitively expensive for some. For example, Patriot Coal Corporation, as part of a landmark settlement concerning such issues, agreed to phase out its surface mining operations altogether.

At the same time, public health researchers have been highlighting the connections between poor human health and communities where mountaintop removal is prevalent. This is even after allowing for public health impacts like diet, smoking, and other such factors.[9] The takeaway, of course, is that it is bad for human health to live in proximity to mountaintop removal operations.

Common Enemies

With the decline in unionization, the scarcity of good-paying jobs in the Appalachian coalfields, and the inevitable backlash to environmental devastation wrought by mining, coal companies often are able to pit workers and environmentalists against each other. Yet these two groups have a common interest and common fate, and thus sometimes find common ground, as in the case of Patriot Coal Corporation.

Patriot Coal is a spinoff company from Peabody Energy. Many industry observers have pointed out that once Patriot Coal was created in 2007, it held many assets which Peabody seemingly wanted to be rid of—namely, unionized operations and operations with a bad environmental record. As a result, Patriot Coal was well positioned to file for bankruptcy to shed itself of obligations to union retirees and avoid massive environmental liabilities. And Patriot has done just that, filing for bankruptcy at least twice as of this writing.

Blankenship's Fall

Over the arc of modern coal industry battles stands a singular, notable development—the trial, conviction, and imprisonment of Don Blankenship for conspiracy to violate federal mine safety laws. In the wake of the Upper Big Branch disaster in April 2010 in which twenty-nine miners died, federal regulators launched an investigation. This was the worst mining disaster in forty years, and the man at the top of the corporate ladder was none other than Don Blankenship.

As the investigation unfolded in the years after the disaster, lower-level Massey Energy executives faced criminal prosecution and conviction. But no such high-level coal executive had ever faced criminal sanction for a disaster like this. However, despite having a high-dollar legal team and seemingly boundless resources to fight the charges, a jury found Blankenship guilty of conspiring to willfully violate federal mine safety laws. While Blankenship wasn't technically convicted for any action that resulted in the Upper Big Branch explosion itself, it nevertheless was an unprecedented legal development, this conviction of a coal executive for a mine safety violation.

Curiously, and tragically, the maximum prison sentence for this misdemeanor conviction for a mine safety violation—with its obvious tie to protecting human welfare—is much lighter than those possible for the other crimes (felony charges of securities fraud and making false statements to financial regulators) of which Blankenship was acquitted. Ultimately, the judge in the case sentenced Blankenship to the maximum allowable prison sentence—one year. It was a mixed, albeit unprecedented, result for prosecutors and the families of the Upper Big Branch victims. Notably, the Beckley *Register-Herald* newspaper, in an editorial, claimed that Blankenship should have been imprisoned for the rest of his life. Undoubtedly, many people close to the Upper Big Branch disaster felt similarly.

Fracking for Gas—New Battle Lines Drawn

A discussion of modern battles in the coal industry would not be complete without recognizing the explosion of oil and gas production in Appalachia in recent years. As with mountain-top removal, market forces and technological developments— along with land and mineral ownership patterns favoring out of state companies—have given rise to an oil and gas industry operating on a scale and scope unprecedented in Appalachia. With horizontal drilling and hydraulic fracturing ("fracking") technology, oil and gas operators have ascended to displace coal production.

As coal faces global marketplace blowback for its role in worsening climate change, cheap natural gas from Marcellus and other deep gas formations presents a seemingly cleaner-burning alternative. However, the environmental and community effects from natural gas production and transmission are many and profound. (And, as research develops, it appears that climate benefits from natural gas are overblown—while it may *burn* cleaner than coal, greenhouse impacts from its production and transmission are becoming better understood.) Communities where deep shale gas operations have mushroomed have been slammed with a host of impacts from industrialization of the countryside—truck traffic, noise, dust, fumes, and impacts to water quality and water quantity. Construction of massive transmission pipelines to get the gas to market compounds the impacts of well pad placement, infrastructure, and production. And, as with coal, those in the community living with the impacts are pitted against workers who land scarce well-paying jobs in rural Appalachia. Distant companies and investors controlling vast swaths of land and mineral wealth oftentimes escape scrutiny and consequence.

The question becomes, if subsequent gas booms hit the Appalachians, whether we can learn from past mistakes in how we handled the boom-and-bust of the coal industry. Will we require companies to conduct themselves more responsibly in the communities where they operate? Will we require them to greatly reduce their greenhouse gas emissions? Will we hold them to higher standards of workplace health and safety? Will we take more ownership of our situation by capturing mineral wealth to help us through the lean times when the inevitable bust happens?

Looking Ahead

It's never been easy to have grown-up discussions in Central Appalachia about the role of coal and other extractive and polluting industries. At highest levels of government, academia, and business, it's not usually acceptable to talk about these industries' external costs. We rarely discuss how these industries have a business model whereby communities and workers bear the operations' negative impacts.

Even more difficult to discuss candidly—and plan for—has been coal's inevitable demise. The numbers don't lie. Even coal executives, economists, and politicians all acknowledge (some more begrudgingly than others) the reality that with declining revenues and stock prices as well as fewer and fewer coal reserves available to mine, the industry will never be what it once was. The result is that state and local budgets, long dependent on coal revenue, are in shambles. Educational systems in the coalfields are a wreck. Many of the most talented among us are leaving the state in droves for greener economic pastures. Hopelessness and drug abuse run rampant.

An entirely different socioeconomic construct lies ahead for Appalachia. The question is whether we are "too little, too late" in planning to tackle these problems. Or can we tap into our Appalachian ingenuity, learn from our mistakes, and chart a viable, more sustainable path forward? Really, the only path to take here is the latter one. Anything less is to concede defeat without even trying to fight for something better. And that's just not who Appalachian people are. For generations, we have been fed a "reality" that there is but one way of doing things—hand in hand with polluting and extractive industry. But we Appalachian people have known better. We have learned hard lessons, persevered, and survived. We are ready to chart our own course.

Notes

1. United States Energy Information Administration, "Natural Gas Expected to Surpass Coal in Mix of Fuel Used for Power Generation in 2016," March 16, 2016, at http://www.eia.gov/todayinenergy/detail.cfm?id=25392 (Accessed May 30, 2017).

2. James M. Van Nostrand, Evan Hansen, and Joseph James, "Expanding Economic Opportunities for West Virginia under the Clean Power Plan," July 21, 2016, at http://energy.law.wvu.edu/files/d/585cffce-0aea-4535-84d0-7344591cfbb8/cpp-phase-ii-final.pdf (Accessed August 2, 2016).

3. Kai T. Erickson, *Everything in Its Path* (New York: Simon & Schuster, 1976), 212–13.

4. "Disaster on Buffalo Creek: A Citizens' Report on Criminal Negligence in a West Virginia Mining Community," at http://media.wvgazette.com/

static/series/buffalocreek/commission.html#anchor716789 (Accessed May 30, 2017).

5.   Bonnie E. Stewart, *No. 9: The 1968 Farmington Mine Disaster* (Morgantown: West Virginia University Press, 2011).

6.   U.S. Department of Health and Human Services, National Institute for Occupational Safety and Health, "Criteria for a Recommended Standard: Occupational Exposure to Respirable Coal Mine Dust," September 1995, at http://www.cdc.gov/niosh/docs/95-106/pdfs/95-106.pdf (Accessed May 30, 2017).

7.   David J. Blackley et al., "Resurgence of a Debilitating and Entirely Preventable Respiratory Disease among Working Coal Miners," *American Journal of Respiratory and Critical Care Medicine*, vol. 190, no. 6, (September 15, 2014), at http://www.blacklungblog.com/wp-content/uploads/2014/09/239746769-Black-Lung-Letter-1.pdf (Accessed May 30, 2017).

8.   See generally Chad Montrie, *To Save the Land and People: A History of Opposition to Surface Coal Mining in Appalachia* (Chapel Hill: University of North Carolina Press, 2003).

9.   Manuel Quinones, "Soft-Spoken Researcher Rattles Appalachian Coal Industry," *Greenwire*, December 13, 2012, at http://www.eenews.net/stories/1059973804 (Accessed May 30, 2017).

Which Path, Appalachia?

Carrie Kline

Carrie Kline holds degrees from the University of Massachusetts Amherst and SUNY Buffalo. She first came to West Virginia in 1984 and fell under the spell of Appalachian legends Don and Connie West at the Appalachian South Folklife Center. She currently operates Talking Across the Lines, a thriving West Virginia small business.

Let's soar above our assumptions of what Appalachian culture is, who fits and how. Let's erase the notions that people can only be a certain way in order to fit in small mountain communities. Let's make room for young people, for artists, and for the young and the artist that lives within us all. And let's use our own power, our belief in ourselves, and our own energy sources for our own good.

> *Timberline*
>
> *Up on the timberline*
> *I took these thoughts of mine.*
> *Take a walk and think about what's been.*
> *Up on the timberline,*
> *Not just wasting time.*
> *Get it straight and head on home again.*
> —David Norris, songwriter

Our coal has been mined, our waters and mountains compromised, and our boom and bust economy is busted. Science and human experience have shown that extraction, processing, and pipelining of oil and gas through the region leads to sickness from air and water, and destabilization of our fragile land, water, and communities. Plus, the market for these extractive resources is as fickle as any other.

This time in Appalachia's history there's no place to flee, no panacea waiting along an out-of-state assembly line. There's nowhere better to land than here if we build upon the best of what we have. We are cooking up a recipe right here, made up of who we were, who we are now, and a vision of how we want to grow.

In West Virginia we now have several avenues for supporting artists and an arts economy through local and regional efforts. We now have solar cooperatives, buying clubs, in many parts of West Virginia, helping people move to renewable energy, and become less beholden to corporate energy companies by placing solar panels on and around their homes. Farmers' markets and farm-to-table efforts have grown.

Appalachia is a natural incubator for small business and cottage industry. We have been nothing if not a people with stick-to-itiveness and ornery determination. We are creative and we make do. We work hard, and on good days we work together.

We are a diverse people with varied skills. We have scratched out a living from the ground, both on it and below it. Even people in wheelchairs and on walkers can share knowledge of skills they once practiced. We have been—and are—farmers, gardeners, miners, loggers, makers of fine steel and glass, workers driving heavy equipment and typing on computer keyboards.

We are industrial workers and fine craftspeople. We have fashioned what we needed, including the houses we live in and the furniture that fills them. Early on we arrived here from nations around the world. To our shame, most Native Americans were forcibly removed or died of European diseases centuries ago. Some few found a way to stay and join in what was to come. In recent years our numbers may have aged and declined, but urban and small town newcomers continue to trickle in, adding their own ways of living to the mix. We Appalachians are of all religions and creeds, shapes and sizes, gender identifications, and sexual orientations.

We have always been artists and makers, innovators. *"Grandpa was a country man. He saw things with his heart. He could take a tall oak tree and turn it into art."* (David Norris, "Timberline") We were a do-it-yourself people long before anyone coined the term "DIY." We had to be. We still have to be.

Our mountains and valleys have been a draw, a magnetic vortex, for people who want to work by hand and by heart, a haven for people who don't want to swim in—or are not welcome in—the current of mainstream commercial and corporate life. People have moved in and stayed, getting elected to school boards, helping mop up and dig out when the floods come, and putting their shoulders to the plow beside neighbors whose people never left, or left and returned.

This is the time to make room for all of us, for the sake of Appalachia's future, for the sake of our children. They want to be here; they want to stay. This can only happen if we create an environment of opportunity and tolerance for creativity and diversity. We have to court our youth and romance our artists, to lay out the red carpet for our own, and for new arrivals who want to fit into our communities—artists, visionaries, and entrepreneurs looking for a safe haven to be and do. Anyone who wants to contribute to the health of our communities is welcome. Tourism is a large contributor to economies worldwide. We can do much more to bring in visitors by merging arts, cultural heritage, and ecotourism. We can repopulate our region with people who wish to live in vibrant arts communities.

Failure to open our minds and hearts will leave a desolate land suitable only as an environmental and human sacrifice zone for the interests of the wealthy who have taken so much and given so little. We don't have to adhere to the same old model of using large extractive industries for our survival. We have the tools. We have done some of the hardest work on earth. We have been survivors. We have been coal miners, boring our way through rock in the dark underground, through gas, water, and fire. We are powerful people. We just need to change the way we think about ourselves. Fear makes us small and closed-minded. Self-confidence makes us soar.

There is something about Appalachia. People from here know it. People who have found this place know it. Retirees who have left for work return to enjoy their later years. That's why we have an older population, made up of people who kept this place in their hearts for decades. People who leave are homesick for the land, the waters, and the people of their childhood. "*In the dead of the night, in the still and the quiet, I slip away like a bird in flight, back to those hills, the place where I call home,*" sang West Virginia native songwriter Hazel Dickens from her Washington, DC, home. Come home, Appalachia. Don't wait until your work years are over. Come home now. Give us the best of what you can offer. Or better yet, stay here to raise your families and your careers. We'll make it as exciting as the cities, with art, music, and nightlife on a smaller scale, and room to be yourself. And we'll protect what's left of our natural beauty, our timberlines and fishing holes. The screen door's open. We've got your bed made up. We've got your coffee saucered and blowed. Pull up to the table.

We can no longer afford to worry about whether someone has been over- or undereducated. Instead, let's teach ourselves to be creative and curious, eager to learn and find meaning in our lives. We need a half a cup of old-time common sense and a half cup of book learning in the recipe for revitalization. To help mend our ravaged land and waters we need scientists and agronomists, and we need traditional stewards who will protect like guard dogs and tend like honeybees. It's too late in our history to fear either the traditional or the modern. We need the best of both.

Let's use our renewable resources. It's time to put solar panels on old mountaintop removal sites, sharing the proceeds cooperatively. And let's produce our own solar panels in Appalachia. Put people to work creating components for renewable energy: wind, solar, and geothermal. A few factories won't solve all our problems, but they'll contribute to our economic transition as we plan our future.

We need all of our minds and our collective wisdom to create sustainable locally owned enterprises. This period at the end of coal gives us an opportunity to take stock of how we want to go forth. Let's assess well and measure local and regional gain for the majority of people before allowing more extraction of water, minerals, and Appalachian people. If we can filter out greed by the wealthy few, our creative initiatives will feed us with food, art, and commerce.

It's passé to focus on where someone was born more than where they are sending down roots. There's no time left on this planet to label ourselves "working folks" versus "tree huggers." We can all be both, without the name-calling. In the floods, droughts, and perils we face, we create local legends of communities coming together across all lines. Heroes rise from the rubble. Artificial divisions were created by those claiming ownership of what rightfully belongs to those who live and work here. The coal industry thrived on divisions among us, profiting from every kind of "othering" they could think of, from different baseball teams to segregated neighborhoods based on culture and language groups. But in forming the UMWA, the walls crumbled. Working people saw common needs and forged solutions through joining together, transcending artificial divisions.

Let's declare the days of division over and done. As we romance our youth and our artists, and the youth and artist in each of us, we must do what we do best. Provide fertile soil for homegrown, small-scale, and cottage industry in arts and every-thing a community needs.

Organize community-owned companies to harness renew-able resources, meeting our own needs wisely and sustainably for the benefit of our own people. Every state and nation has some mix of sun, water, wind, and geothermal energy opportu-nities. They do not need to harvest Appalachia this time. We will cede the forty-hour-plus workweek where we give our time to McDonald's or to a factory, a mine, or a frack job owned by out of state interests with only profit in mind. We can make it with less money, bartering more with sacks of potatoes, with childcare, with music lessons, songwriting, sewing, plumbing, electrical work, and building our own economies with our own know-how mixed with good, caring, outside input. In our transition from nonrenewable finite resources, the health and well-being of our entire community rather than the greed of the few will be the determining factor. We need to wisely steward what remains.

We have homegrown models here: teachers, mentors, heroes. Visitors have come to Appalachia for a long time and continue to flock here for the values we have espoused, our natural and hand-made beauty, and our genuine *hillbilly* ways of communicating (literally Scottish for *friend from the hills*). It's time for us who live here to celebrate our own values of hard work and common visioning. It's time to fully embrace artists, small entrepreneurs, and small-scale economies.

It's time to ungild our herstory and history, to know who to celebrate from our own past. It's time to repair the wrongs of those who came here for their own interests. Leapfrog beyond their models of violence and exploitation. Teach our children well. Enfranchise ourselves with a sense of dignity and determi-nation to flourish.

Let's spend less time parsing through threads of difference, labeling one another. Encourage each other to evolve, to grow, to be each other's inspiration, to be our brother's and sister's keeper. Watch each other's back. Look out for one another. This is the best of traditional Appalachia. Let's keep it up and do a little more.

Our struggle for survival is at least as urgent now as when the organizers of the March on Blair Mountain were on trial for their lives in Charles Town. This is the call: all hands on deck for the survival and flourishing of our land, our waters, our people, and all beings who make this place a home. Work together as a community determined to set our own course. March on.

Connecting the Dots

Wess Harris

OUR PLANET IS BLESSED WITH UNIQUE CULTURES AND LANGUAG-
es that greatly influence not only what we think but also how we
think. This is no big secret but hardly the stuff of everyday conversation. We tend to assume that others think as we do even if
they have opinions that differ from our own. We catch ourselves
asking, "How could they have formed such absurd opinions or
behave in such a crazy manner when *everyone knows* . . .?"

We began this book noting the common perception that the
victors get to write history. We make no apology for pointing to
the errors of much that has been written by mainstream scholars
funded by the very interests keen to continue the subjugation of
our land and people. We have sought to challenge readers with
realities that perhaps they have not encountered elsewhere. What
if more than just the history written but also the very language
used to write it has been controlled by the moneyed interests?
What if they control the very words we use and the worlds we
can imagine? If knowledge is power, then controlling the very
thoughts we think is clearly the mark of the victor. What fear
need the rich have so long as the rest of us cannot even imagine
our world without them?

We all approach each day governed by a collection of assumptions about the world and how it works based on what we have
been taught to accept without question by our parents and teachers. These assumptions are the lenses through which we see the
world. Scientists *assume* that there is some order to the universe;
religious individuals of whatever faith take the existence of God
as a *given*; economists and historians *know* (and teach) that land,
labor, and capital are the sources of value and that growth is necessary for a healthy economy.

The scientist's basic hypothesis of an ordered universe is logical. It makes sense and can, at least in theory, be disproven. Scientists may discover through the use of the scientific method that order does not in fact prevail. The faith of the religious believer is inherently non-logical—it lies outside the framework of logical thought. The postulate of God can be neither proved nor disproved. Both logical and non-logical assumptions offer the possibility of leading us to useful understandings or paths of wisdom. A third approach, illogicality, involves accepting inherently false assumptions as a basis for understanding and can lead only to confusion and the perpetuation of falsehoods.

Regrettably, many economists and historians have built academic careers based on illogical, inherently false assumptions. That they are well paid and tenured for such folly is no accident. The current worldview espoused in our educational system is based on fundamentally false assumptions that define the limits of debate and ensure that no serious challenges to establishment narrative can be entertained. Economics students of today are routinely taught that three sources of value exist: land, labor, and capital. This basic assumption provides the moral justification for the existence of profit or interest—return to capital for its contribution or "value created." The accumulation of vast fortunes thus becomes legitimized. I have never had a student question these sources of value.

Yet capital *is not a source of value*; it is stored value always reducible to an actual source—land (natural resources) or labor. A strong case can be made that human labor alone constitutes the source of all value. *Our labor* is the agency that creates new wealth. We employ land and machines; they do not act alone. Our labor constitutes the source of all wealth.

Stored value, capital, is indeed a necessary component of virtually any viable economy, but logically it is only a *catalyst to production* and not a fundamental source of value. The robber barons of old and the multinational corporations of today provide a social mechanism to concentrate capital, but they do not create the wealth. They control wealth—and all too often the people who create the wealth.

Capital, whether in the form of a hammer, a bulldozer, a factory, or a dollar bill, creates no value; capital creates no wealth. The concentration of stored value (capital) is clearly necessary for any economic development beyond the Stone Age. The problem of just how to ethically, morally, and logically concentrate this stored value for use in economic production is yet to be solved. The important dynamic is that the *owner* of the hammer has created no value yet *demands reward by virtue of ownership.* Siphoning wealth to the already wealthy by virtue of a piece of paper designating them owners of the hammer—or coal mine—only takes food from the tables of those who do create real value, those who actually *work* for their income rather than *own* for their income.

Yet another sacrosanct and clearly illogical assumption built into our culture is belief in the necessity of growth for a "healthy" economy. Virtually all of my students from across the country who have taken basic economics or business classes can readily debate whether a 3 percent or a 6 percent growth rate is indicative of the desired "healthy" economy. Why don't they question the "need" for growth when photos of Earth from space illustrate how finite our resources are?

We all live on a round rock called Earth. It is finite. A growth rate of as much as ½ of 1 percent over time is logically unsustainable and suicidal. The false assumption of the necessity of growth rests squarely upon the equally false assumption that capital is a source of value. Fortunes in the hands of the ultrarich must find some mechanism to return to participation in the economy lest we suffer a dreaded "bust" when too few dollars circulate to purchase goods (value) produced by workers paid less than the value they create. Concentrated wealth in the hands of the owners of capital does not "trickle down" to the rest of us. It seeks ways to grow further, to infinitely expand a capitalist economy that is doomed to collapse if it does not grow. Yet that very mandated growth is logically impossible on a finite planet. The belief that profit is both morally and ethically justified has led us to blindly accept an economic system that is inherently self-destructive. Accepting the false premise that capital is a source of value is leading to the very real possibility that humans will soon no longer be able to inhabit the earth. Infinite growth on a finite planet is a model that does not work.

The perceived desirability of capitalism as an economic system has become pervasive around the world. If we have some basic understanding of the fundamentally illogical nature of the system, why is it held so widely in high esteem by the very people who create value through the sweat of their brow or dancing of fingers on a keyboard only to receive a small pittance in pay? Simply put: capitalism sounds great. Capitalism is marketed to workers who have little sense of their own history and dream of having (and actually working) a business of their own. Some few succeed and join the ranks of the capitalists. Others spend their lives paying steep interest rates to bankers for the loan of funds to start a small business, the capital needed to build the bakery or barber shop.

Ironically, true capitalists—those having sufficient wealth to live on income generated by their possessions rather than their labors—have a strong motivation for opposing the very entrepreneurs whom they tout as the shining stars of capitalism. No sooner has the small first-generation business gained a toehold in the market than larger, established competitors feel compelled to drive them from the playing field. How many dreams of independence have been shattered by the arrival of big-box stores and fast-food chains?

Education, long a trusted path to economic mobility, is increasingly tied to huge student debts. Students are encouraged to improve their usefulness as creators of value but they dare not plan to reap the fruits of their ever-longer hours of labor. Just as immigrants, aspiring miners of a century ago, arrived in coal camps in debt to King Coal for their tools and supplies, today's graduates enter the workforce facing decades of debt. Lives are consumed paying interest on debt tied to learning, tied to aspirations for mobility that will never be realized.

Capitalism in reality is for those who live off the spoils of the wealth, the stored value they control. Capitalism is marketed as a meritocracy when the vast majority of capitalists live off of wealth at best earned by the labor of their ancestors. Capitalism is for those who do not work, not for those who do. That is why it is called capitalism!

The coal camps of old were designed as closed systems of production. The mine, the school, the company store, the scrip, the church, the ball team, the miners and their wives existed only to produce the coal that would become the wealth of the owners, the capitalists. Does the economic globalization mentioned on the evening news simply mean that in the early twenty-first century the entire globe has become as a coal camp of a century ago? Can we better understand the world we live in today by closely examining the social and economic relationships in Whipple, West Virginia, circa 1921?

Perhaps these reflections will be of some small use in separating the wheat from the chaff. Readers are encouraged to consider the offerings presented here through a different lens. An open mind may change for the better the basic assumptions about how our world is to be understood. Perhaps readers can connect the dots exemplified by the articles herein presented to arrive at new levels of understanding. We must regain control of the factual reality of our past. We must also hone the theoretical tools to truly grasp what we often understand intuitively. Knowledge is power. With knowledge comes the understanding that will enable us to rid ourselves of falsehoods and create our own history. Our own herstory. We can create our own story and with it our own future.

Union Miners
Carbondale mine
July 1926

Courtesy of the George Bragg Collection

Gem photo

Coal Owner's Union
Atlantic City
July 1923

Come All You Coal Miners

Sarah Ogan Gunning

Come all you coal miners wherever you may be
And listen to a story that I'll relate to thee
My name is nothing extra, but the truth to you I'll tell
I am a coal miner's wife, I'm sure I wish you well.

I was born in ol' Kentucky, in a coal camp born and bred,
I know all about the pinto beans, bulldog gravy and cornbread,
I know how the coal miners work and slave in the coal mines
    every day
For a dollar in the company store, for that is all they pay.

Coal mining is the most dangerous work in our land today
With plenty of dirty, slaving work, and very little pay.
Coal miner, won't you wake up, and open your eyes and see
What the dirty capitalist system is doing to you and me.

They take your very life blood, they take our children's lives
They take fathers away from children, and husbands away from
    wives.
O miner, won't you organize wherever you may be
And make this a land of freedom for workers like you and me.

Dear miner, they will slave you 'til you can't work no more
And what'll you get for your living but a dollar in a company
    store
A tumbled-down shack to live in, snow and rain pours in the top.
You have to pay the company rent, your dying never stops.

I am a coal miner's wife, I'm sure l wish you well.
Let's sink this capitalist system in the darkest pits of hell.

Sarah Ogan Gunning at Highlander Center.
Photo credit: John Gaventa.

"In a society that can honor Loretta Lynn or Emmylou Harris but not Sarah Ogan Gunning, clearly something is wrong. It means we haven't been able to deal with our roots. We haven't been able to deal with our giants."

—Archie Green, folklorist and labor historian

"We live in capitalism, its power seems inescapable—so did the divine right of kings."
—Ursula K. Le Guin

MONTANI SEMPER LIBERI

Index

Page numbers in *italic* refer to illustrations. "Passim" (literally "scattered") indicates intermittent discussion of a topic over a cluster of pages.

About the Editor

WESS HARRIS IS A SOCIOLOGIST, FARMER, AND EDUCATOR WHO IS widely recognized as a leading authority on West Virginia's Great Mine War. He completed his graduate studies at Ohio University and later worked as a union miner and served as president of L.U. 1555. Each of his three major publications has shed light on previously unknown (oft-censored) history of the coal fields. He currently curates the When Miners March Traveling Museum.

When Miners March

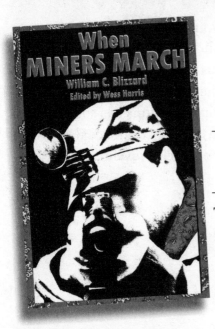

By William C. Blizzard
Edited by Wess Harris

AN INSIDER'S LOOK AT THE
LARGEST OPEN AND ARMED
REBELLION IN U.S. HISTORY

$21.95 • 978-1-60486-300-0 • PAPERBACK •
6x9 • 408 PAGES • LABOR/ HISTORY-U.S.

The uprisings of coal miners that defined the Mine Wars of the 1920s were a direct result of the Draconian rule of the coal companies. The climax was the Battle of Blair Mountain, the largest open and armed rebellion in U.S. history. The Battle, and Union leader Bill Blizzard's quest for justice, was only quelled when the U.S. Army brought guns, poison gas, and aerial bombers to stop the 10,000 bandana-clad miners who formed the spontaneous "Red Neck Army."

Over half a century ago, William C. Blizzard wrote the definitive insider's history of the Mine Wars and the resulting trial for treason of his father, the fearless leader of the Red Neck Army. This is a people's history, complete with previously unpublished family photos and documents. If it brawls a little, and brags a little, and is angry more than a little, well, the people in this book were that way.

"An extraordinary account of a largely ignored but important event in the history of our nation."

—Howard Zinn, author of *A People's History of the United States*

PM Press was founded at the end of 2007 by a small collection of folks with decades of publishing, media, and organizing experience. PM Press co-conspirators have published and distributed hundreds of books, pamphlets, CDs, and DVDs. Members of PM have founded enduring book fairs, spearheaded victorious tenant organizing campaigns, and worked closely with bookstores, academic conferences, and even rock bands to deliver political and challenging ideas to all walks of life. We're old enough to know what we're doing and young enough to know what's at stake.

We seek to create radical and stimulating fiction and non-fiction books, pamphlets, T-shirts, visual and audio materials to entertain, educate, and inspire you. We aim to distribute these through every available channel with every available technology—whether that means you are seeing anarchist classics at our bookfair stalls; reading our latest vegan cookbook at the café; downloading geeky fiction e-books; or digging new music and timely videos from our website.

PM Press is always on the lookout for talented and skilled volunteers, artists, activists, and writers to work with. If you have a great idea for a project or can contribute in some way, please get in touch.

PM Press
PO Box 23912
Oakland CA 94623
510-658-3906
www.pmpress.org

FRIENDS OF PM

These are indisputably momentous times—the financial system is melting down globally and the Empire is stumbling. Now more than ever there is a vital need for radical ideas.

In the many years since its founding—and on a mere shoestring—PM Press has risen to the formidable challenge of publishing and distributing knowledge and entertainment for the struggles ahead. With hundreds of releases to date, we have published an impressive and stimulating array of literature, art, music, politics, and culture. Using every available medium, we've succeeded in connecting those hungry for ideas and information to those putting them into practice.

Friends of PM allows you to directly help impact, amplify, and revitalize the discourse and actions of radical writers, filmmakers, and artists. It provides us with a stable foundation from which we can build upon our early successes and provides a much-needed subsidy for the materials that can't necessarily pay their own way. You can help make that happen—and receive every new title automatically delivered to your door once a month—by joining as a Friend of PM Press. And, we'll throw in a free T-shirt when you sign up.

Here are your options:
- $30 a month: Get all books and pamphlets plus 50% discount on all webstore purchases
- $40 a month: Get all PM Press releases (including CDs and DVDs) plus 50% discount on all webstore purchases
- $100 a month: Superstar—Everything plus PM merchandise, free downloads, and 50% discount on all webstore purchases

For those who can't afford $30 or more a month, we have Sustainer Rates at $15, $10, and $5. Sustainers get a free PM Press T-shirt and a 50% discount on all purchases from our website.

Your Visa or Mastercard will be billed once a month, until you tell us to stop. Or until our efforts succeed in bringing the revolution around. Or the financial meltdown of Capital makes plastic redundant. Whichever comes first.